One with the
UNIVERSE

Finding joy, peace and fulfillment
in everyday living

Dale Furtwengler

FAI Publications
St. Louis, MO

Cover image - Courtesy NASA/JPL-Caltech

Cover design by Nicole Cooper
St. Louis, MO

This publication is designed to provide accurate and authoritative information to the subject matter covered. It is sold with the understanding that the publisher is not engaged in rendering legal, accounting, or other professional advice. If legal advice or other expert assistance is required, the services of a competent professional person should be sought.

Furtwengler, Dale.
One with the UNIVERSE: Finding joy, peace and fulfillment in everyday living/by Dale Furtwengler.

ISBN-978-0692681008
ISBN-0692681000

1.Awareness. 2. Universe. 3. Spirituality. 4. Consciousness. I. Title

Cover illustration by Nicole Cooper, St. Louis, MO, work for hire

TABLE OF CONTENTS

Many paths

There are many paths to any destination. I've had the good fortune to work with a lot of successful people over the years. While these people share common characteristics, rarely have they chosen the same path to success. The same will be true of your journey to become one with the universe.

To illustrate this point, let's think about how you view the universe. Many of you believe that God created the universe, others view the universe as a spiritual nature, still others view the universe as an energy, an essence, in and of itself. What each of these paths have in common is that they recognize the existence of a greater power. We've simply chosen different ways of expressing our view of that power.

Regardless of the path you choose, or whether you switch paths at some later date, *One with the Universe* will help you discover the keys to aligning yourself with that universe. Your reward for achieving that alignment will be a life of joy, peace and fulfillment. More importantly, you'll enjoy these rewards with only a minor adjustment (5 minutes) in your daily routine.

When we think of people who attained heightened levels of awareness, we envision monks and yogis. Their approaches to connect with the universe often involve separating themselves from the distractions of everyday living. They spend countless hours in meditation to clear their minds in order to strengthen their connection to the universe. And it works for them.

But it's not the only path. We overlook people who gain awareness while simultaneously pursuing their aspirations— Mother Teresa, Nelson Mandela, Mahatma Gandhi, Desmond Tutu come to mind.

There's nothing wrong with the approach monks and yogis

1

employ, but it's not the only approach available to you. You can have any life you desire, any career you choose and still gain all of the benefits of being one with the universe. You can find joy, peace and fulfillment in any role you choose. Don't let anyone tell you differently.

In *One with the Universe*, you'll discover that you:

- Are already one with the universe.
- Are connected, but haven't been taught how to use it.
- Can tap into the power of the universe while performing everyday tasks. You don't need a "special routine."
- Have lost your connection to the universe when you experience fear, anxiety, or other negative emotions.
- Can, within seconds, reestablish that connection.
- Will inspire others and help them get through periods of distress.
- Will experience joy and fulfillment in simple tasks and brief encounters with everyone you meet.

Being one with the universe doesn't require you to divorce yourself from society; even monks form communities.

With *One with the Universe* you'll not only enjoy a much larger community, you'll gain joy, peace and fulfillment while you enjoy the activities you, your family and friends treasure. For most of us, that's when we're truly one with the universe— when we're with those we love. Let's begin your journey.

— *Dale Furtwengler*

CHAPTER 1
Already connected

One of the most beautiful aspects of life is that you're always connected to the universe.

You may be wondering "If that's true,

- Why don't I feel that connection?
- Why do I, at times, feel so lost, so alone?
- Why do people spend so much time and energy trying to find that connection if it already exists?
- Why do so many people seem to fail to connect to the universe if they're already connected?"

These are all valid questions. The answers lie in:

1. Proof of the connection.
2. Understanding how to tap into the connection.

In this chapter, by way of your personal experiences, you'll prove to yourself that you're already connected to the universe.

In subsequent chapters, you'll learn how to tap into that connection *at will*, how to regain the connection when you lose it, and why you lose the connection in the first place.

Let's begin by proving that you're already connected to the universe.

Solving problems

I'm certain you've had this experience. You've been trying to solve a problem all day without any success. You go to bed that night still perplexed. You awaken to a solution so obvious you wonder "Why didn't I think of that earlier?"

While the solution seems to have appeared out of thin air, it didn't. It was the result of your subconscious mind working on the problem while you slept. Without realizing it, you asked your subconscious mind (your connection with the universe) to solve the problem and the universe responded with an answer.

Take a few minutes to recall instances like this and you'll quickly realize that it happens consistently. Any time that you go to bed pondering a problem you're facing, you get precisely the same result—an obvious, and often very simple, solution to your problem.

You may be thinking "Yes, I've had that experience. But it's a rare occurrence. It's not something I experience daily." Is that true? Or is it simply a matter that you haven't learned to recognize it when it happens?

As we go on, you'll discover that it's the latter—you don't recognize it for what it is. The remainder of this book will help you gain that awareness and learn how to tap into the power of the universe while going about your daily routine.

We'll get into *how* in the next chapter. At this point you'd probably like more proof that the connection exists. That proof comes in the form of messages the universe is sending. Here are examples of the universe's messages.

New ideas

From out of nowhere an idea pops into your mind. This idea will revolutionize whatever exists today or, at the very least, dramatically improve upon it.

Your subconscious mind (your connection to the universe) is letting you know that you're ready to embark on something that's new, exciting, and has a lot of potential.

Unfortunately, we seldom recognize these ideas as such and, consequently, forgo the rewards the idea affords. I recall being frustrated while driving because a large vehicle directly in front of me prevented me from seeing the brake lights of vehicles ahead of it which slowed my reaction time.

One morning I awoke with the idea of putting break lights in the rear windows of cars, but did absolutely nothing with it. Years later, when rear window brake lights became an industry standard, I couldn't help wondering how much the inventor made off that idea.

When these ideas come to you it's the universe, through your subconscious mind, letting you know that you're ready for bigger, better things. One of the reasons we often ignore these messages is that we can't see how we can make it happen. As a result, we don't pursue the idea with the vigor or rigor it richly deserves.

As with problem solving, you'll learn how to tap into the universe to discover *how* to convert ideas into reality. Before we do, let's look at another proof that we're connected to the universe.

Advising

You're sitting with a friend who is obviously distressed by

a problem she's facing. You listen carefully and, without any prior experience with that issue, provide a solution that is both elegant in its simplicity and provides an immediate solution to the problem.

You not only see this in your dealings with friends, you see it in business when people, who aren't involved in a process, ask questions that shine a light on a better way of doing things. You see it when teachers use examples from other disciplines to make what they're teaching relevant to their students' needs. You also see it when nanoscientists' discoveries trigger medical breakthroughs.

These are all examples of the fact that we're connected to the universe—a higher power, a greater intelligence, however, you choose to describe it. The answers to problems, new ideas and helpful advice come to us from the universe through our subconscious minds—our connection to the universe. In the next chapter we'll discuss the reasons why our subconscious minds are the connection to the universe.

You've had experiences similar to those described above. Wonderful ideas come "out of nowhere," solutions to problems surface "for no apparent reason," you help others "without the benefit of any prior experience in the situation they're facing."

Each of these experiences is evidence of your connection to the universe. The only thing that's been missing, until now, is you're awareness of that connection.

Now that you have proof that you're already connected— proof based on experiences you've had. Let's see how you can tap into that connection more consistently and to greater benefit to you and those whose lives you touch.

CHAPTER 2
Not if, how

"Do or do not. There is no try."—Yoda

I don't know about you, but when I first heard that line my heart leapt with joy. It's so obvious that it's inspiring. Yet like young Skywalker, I couldn't help but wonder "what if I can't?"

It's these doubts that insidiously creep into our minds and deprive of us of the joy we so richly deserve. It's these doubts that:

- Shake your confidence.
- Prevent you from taking advantage of opportunities.
- Cause you to vacillate between doubt and hope, which usually leads to inaction.
- Replace the joy you should be experiencing with fear, anxiety and frustration.
- Prevents you from becoming one with the universe.

These doubts and attendant ill-effects arise because you're asking the wrong question. You're asking yourself *if* you can be successful, you should be asking *how* you can be successful.

Interestingly, as I created the title *One with the Universe*, I was concerned that the title might not resonate with people who

7

possess deeply religious beliefs. In response to that concern I asked the universe "How can I make my message attractive to religious people so that they too can enjoy the benefits of being one with the universe?"

Within minutes the universe suggested *Many paths* for an introduction and back cover text. When I shared this approach with a dear friend and sage advisor, she said "I like it. I love the rich tradition of the religion in which I was raised. I gain a lot of peace and satisfaction from that tradition. Yet I'm often at odds with the teachings of my religion."

Here's the takeaway. When you ask the *how* question, as I did, the universe provides the answer. With that answer come feelings of joy, excitement and a desire to proceed quickly. It's at moments like this that you *feel* connected to the universe or the God that created your universe. In reality, you're connected the whole time. It's just that you don't feel connected while the universe is seeking an answer to your question. As you learn how to tap into the power of the universe, you'll come to *know* that you're connected even though you may not feel it.

Let's see what happens when you ask *if*. Asking *if* puts you at odds with the universe. The universe is great at figuring out how, but when asked if something is possible, it nurtures the doubts and fears implicit in the question. It's the reason why wondering *if* we can be successful results in an endless cycle of doubt, fear, anxiety, hope and the return of doubt. The result typically is inaction or such tentative action as to almost assure that you'll fall short of your goal. Either way, you feel a sense of loss and diminished capacity which almost certainly assures more failures in the future.

How can two words, if and how, create such dramatically different results? Why is one is aligned with the universe while the other is not? Fortunately, there's been a lot of research to help us answer these questions.

Conscious vs. Subconscious

Researchers in the fields of psychology and neuroscience have made fascinating discoveries about the way our minds work. The most significant for our purposes is the delineation between the conscious and subconscious minds.

Scientists prefer the term unconscious to subconscious. I prefer subconscious and will be using it throughout the book. The reason is that, for most lay people, the term unconscious refers to a state brought on by accident or disease whereas the term subconscious implies a fully-functioning individual who has mental processes that aren't observable or fully understood.

While we may not fully understand how the subconscious mind works, we have learned a great deal about its function and how to use it effectively.

In his book, *The Power of Your Subconscious Mind*, Dr. Joseph Murphy, tells us that the subconscious mind has two functions. It manages essential bodily functions like heart rate and respiration and it processes data. He goes on to say that the subconscious mind makes no judgments about the data it is fed, it simply processes the data.

The latter characterization of the subconscious mind helps explain why we get an answer when we ask the *how* question. It also explains why the *if* question generates feelings of fear, doubt, anxiety and frustration.

Implicit in the *if* question is doubt. The subconscious mind is fed the doubt which it processes in a way that perpetuates the doubt, often intensifying it and leading to inaction.

Conversely, a *how* question asks your subconscious mind to find a solution. Your subconscious accepts the challenge and begins working toward a solution. It won't stop until it's found one. Usually that solution is far better than anything you could have imagined consciously.

Aligned with the universe

Another interesting observation about the conscious and subconscious minds comes from Richard E. Nesbitt's book, *Mindware: Tools for Smart Thinking*. Nesbitt says that there is a set of rules that the conscious mind handles readily that the subconscious mind can't. He believes that the subconscious mind also operates by a set of rules, although he readily admits that we don't currently have a clear of understanding of which rules apply to which mind.

Nesbitt's observations about the roles of the conscious and subconscious minds did, however, trigger a thought on another way to consider the two minds we possess in a way that high-lights how well-aligned they are with the universe.

In Einstein's universe, there are hard, fast rules of cause and effect like the gravitational pull on planets that afford us a sense of order which we find satisfying. A few decades later, quantum physics shined a light on a surprisingly chaotic, un-predictable world—one which still begs a unifying theory of the universe.

To me, the conscious mind is equipped to deal with and enjoys order. It's power lies in it's ability to create order. It's through logical thinking that we create that order—the kind of order that's representative of Einstein's universe. It's the mind that creates systems, and thus consistency, in our lives.

Conversely, the subconscious mind is chaotic. It creates connections between seemingly disparate concepts and links them in ways that the conscious mind could never do. That's what makes the subconscious mind such an amazing problem-solving tool. Armed with these insights, let's see what you can do to create better alignment with your universe.

Problem solving

If after a few attempts you aren't making any progress in solving a problem you're facing, set it aside and tackle another task. In other words, assign the problem to your subconscious mind by asking "I wonder *how* I can make this work?" Then go about doing other things. Your subconscious mind will find the solution for you.

You don't have to trust me on this. In Chapter 1, you saw that you've already experienced this phenomenon without fully realizing what was going on. Now that you are aware that your subconscious mind is the more powerful problem solver and that you can tap into it consciously, you have tools you need not only to strengthen your connection to the universe, but to dramatically increase your productivity. For when you stop wasting time trying to solve a problem using logic and divert that energy to tasks where logic is required, you have both your conscious and subconscious minds working to full advantage.

Let's review the process. You assign the problem to your subconscious mind when your conscious mind can't solve it. Your question "*How* can I solve this problem?" acknowledges your awareness that you are connected to the universe and that the universe holds the solution you're seeking. Finally, you realize that what you previously considered happenstance is the result of you having connected with the universe and that you can now connect at will. All you have to do is ask "*How* can I make this happen?"

New insights

I've also discovered that I can consciously tap into my sub-conscious mind to make connections that I wouldn't otherwise make. Here are some examples.

From Brian Greene's *Fabric of the Cosmos* I learned how to use entropy, the second law of thermodynamics, to improve my leadership programs. *The Discipline of Market Leaders* by Treacy and Wiersema helps me price my clients' products and services more effectively. Robert Cialdini's, *Influence: Science and Practice* enables me to help clients sell more effectively.

You get the picture. The way that I gain these insights is, prior to reading these books, I asked my subconscious mind "What am I going to learn that I can use in other aspects of my life?"

It's that simple. By the way, we have a natural tendency to distrust things that seem too simple. The best way I've found to overcome this tendency is to try it. Rather than dismiss the potential of a simple concept, test it. Whether you're reading, watching the discovery channel, engaging in a fun activity, ask your subconscious "What will I learn from this experience that I can use in some other aspect of my life?"

Even when I'm reading James Patterson, Kate Wilhelm or Jeffrey Deavor suspense novels for pleasure, I learn something interesting about human nature. The reason is that just prior to starting the book I ask my subconscious "What am I going to learn from this experience that I can use elsewhere?"

With each experience, your interest in discovering new things heightens. You regain the curiosity you possessed as a toddler. And, like the toddler, the world becomes an amazing place filled with joy and excitement in every endeavor.

With this joy and excitement comes the desire for more. Your desire for more will remind you to ask these questions of your subconscious mind. Asking these questions becomes a habit. This questioning process will become second nature to you—so much so that others will think that you do it naturally. In reality, it was through conscious effort that you developed this habit of tapping into your subconscious.

Everyday activities

I use my subconscious mind in lieu of an alarm clock. I haven't set my alarm in over 25 years. I simply remind my subconscious of the time I need to get up, then go to sleep.

It works just as well when there's a TV program I want to watch. I remind my subconscious of the time the program starts and go about whatever other tasks I intend to do. At roughly five minutes prior to the time the program begins, the thought "It's about time for the program to start" pops into my mind. I have yet to be late getting up or viewing a program I want to see. Your subconscious mind is your connection to the universe. It's potential is limited only by your imagination.

The key is to understand that you can tap into your subconscious at will using your conscious mind. That's the piece of the puzzle that's been missing for most of us. We've never been taught what the subconscious mind can do, much less how to tap into its power.

Takeaway

Your subconscious mind is your link to the universe. You

can access it at will by simply asking it to perform the task you desire whether that's solving a problem, gaining new insights or functioning as an alarm clock. The key is to ask *how, not if* you can achieve the desired goal.

You'll know that you're asking the *if* question when you experience recurring doubt. Everyone experiences doubt, it's an emotion that we can't prevent no matter how hard we try. If, however, that doubt persists—if you can't set it aside quickly— you've lost your connection to the universe. To regain your connection, reframe the question to your subconscious. Don't ask *if* it can be done, ask *how* it can be done. The answer often arrives more quickly than anticipated and you'll once again feel your connection to the universe along with the joy, peace and sense of fulfillment that accompany that connection.

You now know one of the simplest and most effective ways of becoming one with the universe. As you can see, it doesn't require any special knowledge, ritual or alteration to your daily routine to gain this powerful connection. All it takes is asking the right question of your subconscious mind.

In Chapter 3, we're going to explore when to trust your gut. It's something we've all been told to do and have, from time to time, regretted not having done. Let's make that regret a thing of the past.

CHAPTER 3
Trust your gut

If only...

Years ago I applied for a job with a CPA firm—one that I thought had quicker partnership potential than the firm I was with.

Despite having done extensive research on my prospective employer I had a feeling that I was missing something—something didn't feel right. Because I couldn't find a logical reason why I shouldn't, I took the job. Within five months of having accepted the position I was looking for another job. From that experience, I learned to trust my gut.

I'm not unique in my regret. I've heard stories from countless people who regret not trusting their gut. Some regrets, like mine, involved jobs that shouldn't have been taken, others were missed opportunities, still others were relationships that should have been avoided.

Regardless of the regret, in each instance the person felt as if he were about to make a mistake, yet couldn't put his finger on the source of his discomfort and, consequently, made a bad decision.

In order to understand why this happens, we need answers to the following questions:

- What is this mysterious gut?
- Why does it send these signals?
- Why aren't we paying attention?
- How can we overcome this unproductive tendency?

What is this mysterious gut?

You're already ahead of me on this one. You know that it's your subconscious mind's connection to the universe. It's the universe telling you that something is amiss. Your subconscious mind is the conduit for signals you get from the universe.

You've had this experience. You sense that the driver next to you is about to do something stupid *before it happens*. This "sixth sense" prevents an accident.

Despite being intensely focused on what you're doing, you sense someone's presence. Upon seeing slight changes in body language or the tone of a person's voice you anticipate and are able to prepare for challenges to your idea.

"Gut feelings" are further evidence of your connection to the universe. Your subconscious is constantly monitoring your environment—bodily functions as well as problems that need solving and ideas (opportunities) that are aligned with where you are in your personal and professional development.

Now that we know what your gut is, let's figure out why we get these signals in such a seemingly untrustworthy manner.

Why do we get these signals?

The answer is that if we tried to *consciously* monitor all the things our subconscious mind does, we'd quickly overwhelm our conscious minds.

Think of your conscious mind as the engine of your car. As you increase speed or add to the load your hauling, your engine has to increase the rounds per minute it turns to meet increasing demands. If you continue to accelerate or increase the load, the engine bogs down and begins to overheat. Unless you relieve some of the pressure your engine will ultimately fail, it'll shut down completely.

At the time I was writing this chapter, I was in the audience as my dear friend, Dr. Dan Fazio, talked about the subconscious mind. He cited neuroscientists' studies which indicate that the conscious mind processes data at a rate roughly equivalent to a computer speed of 30 to 60 bits per second.

The consensus among these neuroscientists is that the total processing power of the brain is somewhere in the vicinity of 20 *million* bits per second. This disparity in processing rates is an indication of how much more powerful your subconscious mind is over your conscious mind in processing data.

You know this from personal experience. Despite all the talk of multi-tasking, you know how draining it is when you try to sustain that level of activity. You also know that the volume of mistakes go up dramatically the more you attempt to multi-task. It's the reason why ad campaigns, fines, and penalties are directed at people who text while driving. There's increasing evidence that while we think ourselves capable of doing two things at once, we don't do them very effectively and, at times, put ourselves and others at risk in attempting to do so.

Because the subconscious mind takes on essential tasks and performs them automatically, you have the ability to focus your conscious mind on whatever task you choose with an intensity that wouldn't otherwise be possible.

This separation of duties and the "invisible" nature of the subconscious mind's workings are what cause the subconscious mind's messages to appear as "gut feelings." These feelings are often viewed as intrusions upon what our conscious mind is considering. Because, until now, you haven't been aware of the source or reliability of these feelings, you distrusted them, often to your chagrin.

Armed with an understanding of why we get these signals and why we tend to distrust them, let's figure out how to overcome this debilitating tendency.

Trusting your gut

For me, learning to trust was a matter of recognizing how frequently my gut was right. Examples surfaced in all aspects of my life.

I found myself sensing danger before there was any reason to expect it. During intensely-focused activities, I'd sense a presence before I was aware that the person was there. I'd be drawn to an idea only to discover a lesson I would never have anticipated. Here's an example to illustrate this last point.

I had some time on the weekend and was looking for something to read that was different. I didn't have anything in mind, I just wanted something different. I went to the library. While browsing the stacks in search of something intriguing, I came across a book entitled *Playing Ball on Running Water* by David Reynolds.

As soon as I saw the title I thought "I've got to know what this is about." Reynolds is a psychotherapist who studied both in the United States and Japan. In *Playing Ball* he noted that the primary difference between the East and West is that, in the West, we strive to understand why people behave as they do. In the East they don't care about why, they simply help their patients change their behaviors.

I not only found this intriguing, but useful in my consulting and coaching business. I realized that when I ascribed motives to my clients behavior, I was usually wrong in my assessment.

Now, rather than wasting a lot of time and energy trying to figure out why my clients are doing what they're doing, I help them develop behaviors that produce better results.

Using this new approach my clients are able to get results more quickly *and* increase their confidence. In the past, my "western" approach would have put them through the risky exercise of examining their motives and behaviors—opening the door to a sense of inadequacy if not outright failure.

This gain can be attributed to the universe letting me know that I needed to pursue something different without giving me a clue as to what that difference should be.

I trusted my gut. I went to the library, not with a plan, but to explore possibilities. I was rewarded handsomely for the trust I placed in the universe. When you learn to trust your gut —to act on messages the universe is sending—you'll enjoy similar results.

You've had similar experiences. What's been missing is your awareness of what's happening. Now that you understand how the universe works and your connection to it, it'll be easy for you to recognize the messages that'll make your life, and the lives of those around you, richer and more fulfilling.

Takeaway

Your "gut" is further evidence of your connection to the

universe. The way to learn to trust your gut is to:

1. Become aware of how often you get messages from the universe.
2. Pay attention to how accurate these messages are.

Every danger signal, every dream, every aspiration, every solution is a message from the universe. Instead of ignoring these messages, as we both have in the past, act on them and you'll be amazed at the wonderful things that happen.

With each experience you'll learn to trust the messages you receive. You'll act upon these messages more quickly and with greater confidence. It'll become second nature for you to act— you won't think about it, you'll simply follow your inclination (what your gut is telling you) even when the message is vague as was my desire for "something different."

In the future, instead of thinking "If only...," you'll enjoy success and joy that others dream of possessing—all because you've learned to trust your gut.

At this juncture, I'd be surprised if you weren't thinking. "I've tried a lot of things in the past and none of them worked, why should I believe that what you're suggesting will be any different?"

Great question! In the past, I tried a lot of things with little success. In the following chapter, I'll share what I discovered.

CHAPTER 4
Action!

All of my failed attempts to connect with the universe had one thing in common, they lacked proper action.—Yours truly.

Over the years my attempts to connect with the universe have included prayer, meditation, visualization, and a host of other avenues all of which I found lacking. Yet, I know people who enjoy great success with these approaches and am thrilled for them.

If they're working for you, keep doing them. As I said at the beginning of this book, there are many paths to any given destination. For those of you who, like me, have found results disappointing, here's what I learned.

Prayer

I discovered that the reason why I was failing to "get an answer to my prayers" is that I was praying for the result, not a path to the result. In other words, I wanted God or the universe to solve my problem for me—to fix whatever I wanted fixed.

Ain't happening! My experience is that the universe will shine a light on the path for me, but it's up to me to move down that path. I have to take action or nothing happens.

The same is true for you. You need to take action to get the result you desire. If you don't, you forgo whatever you might have gained from taking that action.

Meditation

Again it's probably my mistaken perception of meditation, but I wasn't getting the result others enjoyed.

My attempts involved sitting quietly in the traditional lotus position and controlling my breathing in an attempt to free my mind so that I could enjoy connecting with the universe.

It didn't work for me. My connections would come when I propped my feet on the desk or stretched out on the sofa and let my mind wander. The results were amazing.

New ideas would surface as would solutions to problems I was facing. I'd get ideas on how to present my messages more effectively, how to improve relations with clients, students and colleagues or how to do something special for family members.

My "meditations" were always productive and rarely took more than 15 minutes to produce a result. The key is to give myself permission to allow my mind to wander aimlessly. It's that action that made "meditation" work for me.

A number of people who have had success with meditation all agree that what I'm doing is a form of meditation—one that fits my nature. It's another reason why I'm writing this book—to dispel the myth that you have to follow traditional methods.

With meditation my disappointment didn't result from a failure to take action, but from taking action that was contrary to may nature. We'll discuss this more in Chapter 6, *Fighting nature*.

The Secret

I'm sure most of you are familiar with either the book or the movie, *The Secret*. Both encourage you to visualize your success—to see yourself enjoying the rewards of that success. I tried; it didn't work for me. As I searched for an explanation for my lack of success I realized that, like prayer, while I was visualizing success, I wasn't taking action to make it a reality. Absent the action, I was never going to experience the success I envisioned.

As you can see, the common theme in all of these failed attempts was either a lack of action or actions that didn't fit my nature. With prayer, I was asking for a fix instead of guidance. With meditation, I didn't give my mind permission to wander. I was trying to force it to do something that didn't feel natural. With visualization, I again was looking for a result instead of guidance on how to gain the result.

Your willingness to take action is directly related to your desire for the result. There are things you've dreamt of doing, things you desired, things you wanted to explore but never did. Why? Because you lacked the desire to take action...or was it a lack of confidence? Let's explore these questions.

Desire or confidence?

As you recall lost or forgone opportunities, here are some thoughts that crossed your mind "I really wanted...but I wasn't confident enough to take action; I was afraid of failing; I didn't think it was possible; I couldn't imagine how I could make it work." In your mind, these thoughts are indications of a lack of confidence. Is that true?

Here's what I've observed. When people want something badly enough, nothing will stand in their way including a lack of confidence. In fact, as I outlined in my book, *Lead a Life of Confidence: Free yourself of fear, anxiety and frustration,* I was a very shy, insecure child despite having grown up in one of the most encouraging, nurturing home environments possible.

Even before I understood what I shared with readers in that book, I wasn't dissuaded by my doubts, fears and anxiety—and there were always plenty of them in existence *even though my desire was strong.*

Take a moment to reflect on the success you've enjoyed over the years, whether that success is personal relationships, career advancement or business success. What you'll recall is that you:

- Had doubts about whether or not it would work.
- Weren't sure what was required to be successful.
- Had only an inkling of how to get started.
- Yet, were certain that you needed to pursue this path.

Now if that list, or my experience in moving from shy, insecure child to gregarious adult, don't substantiate the power of desire to overwhelm a lack of confidence, I don't know what does. In the next chapter we're going to explore the elements of desire and how to evaluate and utilize desire to help you be one with the universe.

Before we do, let's review what we've learned.

Takeaway

I doubt that anyone has more eloquently stated the need for

action than Napoleon Hill in his book *Think and Grow Rich*. He says:

> *"Knowledge will not attract money unless it is organized and intelligently directed through practical plans of action to the definite end of accumulation of money.*
>
> *Lack of understanding of this fact has been the source of confusion to millions of people who falsely believe that 'knowledge is power.' It is nothing of the sort!*
>
> *Knowledge is only potential power. It becomes power only when, and if, it is organized into definite plans of action and directed to a definite end."*

While Hill's focus is on producing wealth, his message is equally applicable to personal development and humanitarian efforts. Regardless of what "definite end" you choose, the key to your success lies in action. You must take action or nothing will happen. When you take action, the universe provides the resources you need to accomplish your goal.

To illustrate this point, as I was writing this chapter my friend, Bill Prenatt, unaware of what I was doing, sent me the Napoleon Hill quote which fit perfectly with my message. As Bill says "We couldn't script stuff to work out this well." And he's right!

Fortunately you don't have to script it, the universe does it for you. The only two things the universe requires is that you pay attention to its messages and take action to achieve whatever end you choose.

As I mentioned a moment ago, willingness to take action is directly related to the level of desire you possess. It's time to discover the secret to evaluating and effectively utilizing desire to make more informed decisions.

CHAPTER 5
Evaluating desire

Desire is the measuring stick the universe has provided to help us make more informed decisions.

In some respects, desire mimics the chaos of the subatomic universe. It's at times irresistible; at other times fleeting. It can spawn hope, excitement and fuel great discoveries or engender fear, anxiety, frustration and inaction.

There have been times in your life that you've felt drawn to an opportunity or activity. You couldn't explain why, but every waking moment your thoughts drifted back to that opportunity. It's draw was irresistible.

Whatever that draw was, it sparked feelings of excitement, hope, and joy. The world became fun again. You felt like a kid awaiting Santa's arrival—the energy you experienced made it difficult to sleep. Because it was fun, you didn't mind.

Not every idea produces that effect. You've also had ideas that sparked the thought "That'd be cool," but nothing beyond that reaction. It's as if you dismissed the idea as quickly as it arrived. In essence you did, often without understanding why. The idea just didn't have enough appeal to hold your attention.

Before we attempt to understand why we have these two distinctly different experiences, let's explore the doubts, fears,

anxiety and frustration that failed attempts produce.
   Who among us hasn't:

- Felt the pain of having pursued an irresistible idea only to find it more difficult than anticipated?
- Had their confidence shaken as a result?
- Feared failure and become anxious over whether or not to proceed?
- Been frustrated by nagging doubts, fears and anxiety?
- With each disappointment, become increasingly reluctant to subject ourselves to further disappointment?

   The key to better experiences is understanding that desire is a measuring stick that enables us to make conscious decisions during the pursuit of any idea that intrigues us.
   As we discussed in the opening of this chapter, desire can be intense or fleeting, growing or waning. Regardless of which of these emotions you're experiencing, the key is to understand the desire you're experiencing so that you can make informed decisions about whether to pursue an idea, or abandon it for a better alternative. That'll be the focus of the remainder of this chapter—learning to use desire to make informed decisions.

Understanding desire
   Desire is:

- An emotional reaction.
- Dynamic—it moves along a spectrum from fleeting to irresistible.
- A useful measure of whether or not you should proceed.

- A great way to minimize fear, anxiety and frustration.
- The key to persevering when things aren't going well.

Emotional reaction

Saying that desire is an emotional reaction doesn't mean much until we realize that emotions are automatic responses. We can't prevent them. Nor should we try; our emotions are part of our survival mechanism. However, absent a threat to our well being, emotions can and should be managed in ways that produce better results for us. We want emotions to enrich rather than diminish the feelings of joy, fulfillment, and peace we experience.

As we become more aware of our desires, as well as how and why they change, the better we become at deciding which desires to pursue and which to forgo.

You'll soon discover how to use this awareness to measure your desire and make more conscious decisions about what you want in life. In doing so, you'll rid yourself of the fear, anxiety and frustration that plague so many of us.

Later in the chapter, you'll see examples of how this works. For now, let's explore the dynamic aspects of desire.

Dynamic

To get a sense for the dynamics of desire, let's explore an experience everyone has had—a great idea.

Without warning an amazing idea pops into your mind. It's new, exciting, full of potential and something you'd dearly love to do. Your desire is intense, the idea irresistible.

You explore the idea with all of the joy and excitement of a toddler with a new toy. Any time that your mind is free, your thoughts return to the idea. You're looking for ways to convert that idea into something tangible—something useful.

You expect obstacles; you know they're inevitable. Indeed, part of the allure is knowing that you'll be testing yourself to see how creative you can be. As time wears on, as challenges mount, as you begin to doubt whether the idea is feasible, your desire wanes.

You awaken more with dread than excitement for the new idea. Your confidence is shaken. You begin to feel that you're wasting your time—that you're tilting at windmills.

Then you make a breakthrough and the excitement returns, doubt is replaced by confidence, fear by optimism, dread by an irresistible attraction. More obstacles surface, doubts creep in, the goal line seems even more distant and elusive. Again, your interest and desire wane. Doubts, fears, anxiety and frustration resurface. The cycle continues until you either give up on the idea or persist through sheer force of will to make it happen.

Unfortunately, the longer that it takes to convert your idea into something useful, the greater the likelihood you'll give up. You've often been told, and you've often observed, that people give up shortly before getting to the finish line.

The tragedy lies not only in forgoing your idea, but in the impact it has on future ideas. When you give up on an idea, you increase the likelihood that you'll do so again, only more quickly than you did previously. Even more devastating is the fact that you'll live with the disappointment, fear and anxiety that linger long after your decision to quit.

There is a cumulative, negative effect on your psyche with every "failed" attempt. In other words, once you've given up on a dream, it becomes easier to give up on future dreams. So much so that you quickly dismiss future ideas that could and should be pursued. In the process, you deprive yourself of the joy, peace and fulfillment you so richly deserve.

We're not going to let that happen again. Instead, you're going to discover how to use desire to make conscious choices. For it's in conscious rather than emotional choices that we can abandon ideas without experiencing all the negative emotions outlined above.

Measuring desire

We can quickly dispense with the lower end of the desire spectrum—that part of the spectrum that runs from "Cool idea, not interested" to "Interesting, but not worth the effort."

Eliminating the low end of the desire spectrum makes it easier to deal with desires that inspire you to act. You'll learn to measure the intensity of the desire you're experiencing to see whether you should act upon it. More importantly, you'll make the decision consciously.

The problem with our "normal" decision-making process is that it is emotional. Something interests us so we charge ahead without regard to what's required. When challenges surface, as they inevitably do, we begin to question not only whether it's worth continuing to pursue the idea, but whether we have the ability to be successful.

With each new challenge doubts intensify, your confidence takes a hit, you fear that you're in over your head, you become more inclined to give up. All of these negative emotions are the byproduct of having made an *emotional* decision.

When you learn how to evaluate desire early in the process,

you'll find that you're able to make more conscious, reasoned decisions and avoid the pitfalls of emotional decisions.

On the surface, this last bit of advice may seem to fly in the face of Chapter 2's message, trust your gut. It doesn't. There's a distinction between messages of impending danger and new ideas. You don't want to ignore the universe's warnings that something is amiss. As you know from personal experience, ignoring these warnings almost always leaves you regretting your decision.

New ideas are the universe's messages of possibility. You are alerted to the fact that you have the potential to convert an idea into something new, exciting, and revolutionary. As with the warnings, the choice is yours. While conscious decisions to ignore warnings are almost always regretted, conscious choices to forgo opportunities can be energizing and uplifting. Here's a personal example to illustrate my point.

I was the CFO of a mortgage banking firm. I was making good money and enjoyed my job, but I wasn't making as much money as the young man who was involved in funding hospital deals. I take no pride in admitting that I was envious.

My envy led to dissatisfaction with my job and income. I began to wonder whether or not I could be as successful as this young man in generating hospital deals.

Note: At that time I wasn't aware of the "Not if, how" concept. If I had been, I would've realized that I would be successful *if it was something I truly desired*.

As I reflected on the things this young man had to do to be successful, I quickly realized that they weren't things I enjoyed. I made a conscious decision not to pursue this career path.

Instantaneously, the satisfaction I previously experienced returned. The key was that I enumerated, to the best of my ability, what was needed to enjoy success in a new role *prior* to taking any action. In other words, I evaluated my desire in advance of taking action.

The *conscious* decision to forgo a career that might have been more financially lucrative replaced my feelings of envy and dissatisfaction with those of joy, peace and fulfillment.

That's the benefit of evaluating desire early in the decision-making process. Now that you know the benefit, let's discover how to make that happen in your life.

Irresistible desires

These are the thoughts to which your mind returns every waking moment whenever your mind is free. No matter how hard you try to dismiss the idea, it permeates your very being.

While the strength of your desire is a powerful indicator that this is a direction in which you should move, it's in your best interest to evaluate what you'll need to do to be successful.

The key is to ask *"How* am I going to make this happen?" Remember, your subconscious mind is flawless in its ability to provide the answer to this question. When you ask your sub-conscious *whether* you'll be successful, you sow the seeds of doubt and insecurity which your subconscious mind nurtures and perpetuates.

One other thing to remember is that with irresistible desires it's likely that when you ask "How...." the answer will include only the first few steps you need to take. Personally, I have yet to have the answer come to me in the form of a full-blown action plan. It's never worked that way for me, nor for my dear friend, Stephanie Hieken.

She said "The first few steps I need to take are always very clear, as is the endgame. It's the stuff in the middle that's vague and murky." She then said "The middle becomes more clear if you're listening, and you are open to the idea that the endgame may not be the endgame you envisioned." The openness she describes is one of being open to the messages of the universe.

While it would be nice to have a full-blown plan, as long as the first steps are things you're willing to do to achieve the goal —do it. Just make sure that as each subsequent step becomes clear, you reevaluate your desire to continue.

Strong desires

The pull, the attraction of a strong desire is obviously not as strong as an irresistible desire. Instead of your mind being continuously drawn back to the idea, which is the hallmark of an irresistible desire, an idea that generates a strong desire will surface periodically, usually when a related idea surfaces.

While the intensity of the desire is different, the approach for evaluating the desire is precisely the same. Ask the *how* question. As long as you're willing to take the first steps—as long as you're making that decision consciously—you'll be happy. You need to reevaluate your desire as each new step or series of steps surface—and you need to choose consciously.

Moderate desires

If an idea intrigues you but you're not sure whether or not you want to pursue it, you probably shouldn't. One of the most important lessons I've learned over the years is that converting an idea into something useful is always more difficult than I anticipate *and* it takes much longer to achieve than I envision. Most worthwhile goals take more than a decade to achieve.

If you doubt that, listen to what highly-successful people say. Garth Brooks upon becoming famous was asked "How does it feel to be an overnight success?" He responded, "Not bad considering it took 14 years."

Tiger Woods reportedly took an interest in golf at the ripe old age of six *months* and appeared on television demonstrating his swing at age two.

Most olympic athletes begin at very early ages and practice relentlessly, through pain and injury, for an opportunity that presents itself only once every four years.

Physicists devote their entire lives to answering questions that are unlikely to be answered in their lifetimes.

This isn't just true for the rich and famous, it's equally true for all of us. If you look at anything worthwhile that you've achieved and what you had to do to achieve that success, I'm certain that you'll find your success was the result of efforts that spanned a decade or more.

Success always takes more time, energy and perseverance than we realize. That's why I'm suggesting that if you're only moderately interested in something, you make a conscious decision to forgo it. That conscious choice will not only save you a lot of wasted time and energy, you'll avoid the inevitable feelings of frustration, doubt and anxiety that surface because you're not doing what you need to do to be successful.

You've been down that road before. You know what it's like to establish a goal only to find your interest waning to the point that you're no longer doing the things you need to do to be successful in that endeavor. You know the impact that it has on your confidence, on your attitude, your behaviors. It's toxic.

You can avoid these negative effects by making conscious choices to forgo ideas that are only moderately interesting.

Takeaway

Before pursuing an idea that intrigues you, evaluate your desire. If your desire is on the low-to-moderate range on the spectrum, dismiss the idea immediately. Save your time and energy for one that triggers a strong, if not irresistible, desire.

You can assess your desire by asking "How can I convert this idea into something useful?" The universe responds with the initial steps you need to take. If you look forward to taking these steps, act now! If the steps feel like chores, or if you find yourself wondering whether it's worth the effort, forgo the idea.

Regardless of which of these feelings you're experiencing, make your choice consciously. You'll experience greater joy when you evaluate your desire *before* embarking on a new adventure.

Now that you have some tools for evaluating desire, let's turn your attention to a natural tendency we all possess—the tendency to fight our nature.

CHAPTER 6
Fighting nature

Resistance is futile, as is misdirected persistence.

We human beings have a nasty habit of fighting our nature. We tend to resist the things that come naturally to us and persist in attempting things that don't. Here are a couple of examples that illustrate this point.

Misdirected persistence

I was recently introduced to a woman who has had a lot of success using podcasts and video in her business. She told me that she'd been working on a book for over two years, then she confessed that she was "resisting" writing her book.

What she failed to realize is that the reason she's resisting is that writing neither comes naturally to her, nor is something she enjoys. In fact, it's so low on her desire spectrum that she is unlikely to ever complete the task.

As long as the book remains unfinished she'll feel anxious. She'll feel that she's not doing something she should do. Even worse, with each passing week and month, she'll question her ability which will diminish her confidence.

If, through sheer force of will, she does complete her book, the result isn't likely to be very good. It'll have been a chore instead of a labor of love. When we're faced with chores, we tend to do them quickly, often with little concern over how well we've completed the task. That's not a formula for success.

The resistance she is feeling is the universe's way of telling her that she's fighting her nature. The joy she finds in creating podcasts and videos is the universe's message that she's being true to her nature.

Resistance

A dear friend, who is both an astute business person and very devote Christian, said that for years she'd been trying to keep her religious beliefs and business separate.

Recently she discovered a way to blend them that enables her to be true to all aspects of her nature and provide a better result for her business clients.

As she was sharing this revelation to a group of us she said, "For years Dale has been telling me that if it feels right, I know I'm on the right path. This feels right."

Unfortunately, when I made that statement, I didn't have the level of awareness (understanding) that I do today. If I had, instead of saying "If it feels right you know you're on the right path." I could have explained to her why that was true. That it was the universe telling her that she should be blending the two —that she and her clients will enjoy greater success when she does. I would've been able to explain why resistance is futile.

The good news is that she gained these insights from a mutual friend who communicated the concept more eloquently than I did. The universe always provides what we need, when we ask the right questions.

Alignment

When we stop fighting our nature, we align ourselves with the universe. When we're aligned, life is fun and exciting.

The opposite is true when alignment is missing. Absent alignment we experience frustration, doubts, anxiety and fear. What you feel is an amazing barometer of how well you've aligned your nature and the universe.

Takeaway

Resistance is a sign that you're fighting your nature. If you resist doing something you feel you should be doing, look for an alternative way of accomplishing your goal. The woman in the misdirected persistence section was fighting her nature by trying to write a book. Creating an audio book would achieve her goal of getting published, but would do so in a form that fit her nature—podcasts and videos.

If you're avoiding something that comes naturally to you, the universe lets you know by regularly presenting the idea to you. I have no doubt that the friend who attempted to keep her religious beliefs and business values separate had, on numerous occasions, experienced the thought that she should be blending the two. Yet she resisted.

Whether you're resisting an irresistible idea or persisting in doing something you don't enjoy, you'll experience frustration, disappointment and malaise. Remain true to your nature and you'll experience excitement, joy, peace and fulfillment.

Now that you're aware of your connection to the universe and how to use it to your advantage, let's apply this knowledge to everyday living.

CHAPTER 7
Everyday living

The universe continuously sends us messages, unfortunately no one has taught us how to interpret them...until now.

Before we get into how to interpret the universe's messages it's important to note that the universe merely suggests, it does not dictate. It suggests solutions to problems, courses of action, bold ideas that indicate your readiness to implement them, and warnings of impending danger.

You can choose to act upon these suggestions or not. The choice is yours and yours alone to make. Once you've made your choice, you'll get feedback on that choice. Make the right choice and you'll experience joy, peace, exhilaration, gratitude, and a desire to share your good fortune with others.

Make the wrong choice and you'll know that as well. You will procrastinate as your feelings repel you from the task that awaits you. The more you postpone the dreaded task, the more irritable you become. You don't like yourself very much. You feel weak and undisciplined. You feel exhausted, and you are! Fighting your nature is exhausting work.

In the remainder of this chapter, we're going to ignore the times when you've made the right decision. In making these decisions you became one with the universe; there's nothing for you to do but enjoy the positive energy that connection creates.

We're going to focus on the times when you've lost your connection to the universe. You're going to discover why you lose your connection and, more importantly, how to regain that connection within *seconds* of having lost it.

Obviously I'm not going to be able to cover all the possible situations you might face. I am going to cover those that I find occurring most frequently in peoples' lives.

One more note before we begin. Throughout this chapter, we're going to discuss negative emotions and your contribution to these negative feelings. You might feel that I'm suggesting that everything is your fault. That's certainly not the case.

In *Stand Out From The Crowd* I readily acknowledge that I contribute to every problem I face, as do we all. That isn't the same as being solely responsible for the problem. When you're willing to acknowledge your contribution to the problem, you become one with the universe, and open the door to solutions that will return you to a life of joy, peace and fulfillment.

Assuming full responsibility leads to feelings of diminished value, which limits your value to yourself, those you love, and those who could benefit from your help. In other words, you lose your connection to the universe.

In the following *everyday-living* examples, you'll become aware of situations that regularly occur in your daily activities. As you explore each of these situations, you'll discover:

- The emotions associated with each message.
- What that means for your connection to the universe.
- What actions to take.

We'll begin with one of the most compelling desires we

possess—the desire to control.

Control

One of the things we naturally desire is control. The desire to control our own lives begins roughly at age two and becomes more pronounced as we grow older and gain experience.

The reality is that we can't control anything other than our own behavior. If we understood this, we wouldn't waste time and energy trying to control things that we can't control. We wouldn't attempt to control the behaviors of our kids, friends, employees and colleagues. We wouldn't try to convince others to change when they don't want to change.

You may wonder "Don't I have a responsibility to my kids, my family, my friends and all I meet to help them avoid choices that are not in their best interests?"

Your responsibility is to make them aware of the risks they face, while respecting their right to make their choices *whether you agree with those choices or not.*

You know how much you resent others telling you you're wrong, you're making a mistake, you'll irreparably damage yourself if you proceed. You don't mind them expressing their concern and offering other perspectives. What you despise is their insistence that they're right and you're wrong. You hate the fact that they desire to control you— their unwillingness to respect your right to the choice you've made.

On the flip side, you know how miserably you've failed when you tried to control things you can't control. You also know that the more you try to control other people's behavior, the more they resist *in precisely the same manner you do.* Your inability to convince others to change in a way you desire leads to feelings of anxiety, fear, frustration and helplessness. These emotions are indications that you've lost your connection to the universe.

Here's how you can regain your connection. Shift from control to influence. Over the years I've discovered:

1. I can't control others, but I can influence them.
2. When I try to control I feel stressed, anxious, frustrated, and, at times, angry, exhausted, and a failure.
3. When I try to influence, I enjoy greater success as well as the attendant feelings of exhilaration, confidence, excitement, optimism, and gratitude.
4. Even when my attempts to influence fail, I enjoy peace knowing that, like the universe, I can only suggest. The choice lies with the other person...as it should.

Let's explore the difference between control and influence by looking at situations in which we often feel compelled to control others' behavior.

Controlling your child's behavior

You want your child to keep his room clean. You tell him that he's got to have his bed made and toys put away before he goes to school.

Despite repeated reminders and threats he does neither, or does them only occasionally. With each reminder, your child's resistance grows—none of us likes being told what to do. With each failure, you intensify efforts to gain control—to get him to "respect" your wishes. The more you press, the more he resists until the situation gets completely blown out of proportion.

You both feel stressed, anxious, and adamant in your belief that you're right. Your minds close to alternatives as each of you insists upon imposing your will on the other. Both of you miss the love and joy you previously experienced, yet you feel powerless to resolve the situation.

These negative emotions and sense of loss are signs that you've lost your connection to the universe. It's a sign from the universe that you need to change your approach.

Unfortunately no one has taught you how to read that sign much less what to do about it. If they had, you'd know that the first thing you want to do is recognize that we're all different.

Some of us are morning people, others function better late at night. It may be that your son is resisting because he's not a morning person. Getting up a few minutes early to make his bed and put his toys away is unconscionable. He'd be fighting his nature. It could be that he doesn't like a regimen—that he prefers a more fluid schedule.

The second thing you need to understand is that the reason doesn't matter. The solution to avoiding this kind of dispute is to influence behavior instead of trying to control it. The way that you influence others' behavior is to offer them options, any of which are acceptable to you.

In this situation, ask your son whether he'd prefer to clean his room before he goes to school, immediately upon returning from school or some other time during the day.

The key is to give him choices about *when* to do what you want, not *if* he does it. The simple act of giving him choices allows him to feel that he has some control over his life which makes it easier for him to honor your request.

Of course there have to be consequences if he fails to honor his commitment. My experience has been that when I remind a person that his commitment is the choice he made, he honors his commitment. Most of us instinctively know—our message from the universe—that life is easier and much more enjoyable when we honor our commitments.

As you can see, the key is to offer choices that will satisfy your desire and allow the other person to choose, then hold the person accountable for his choices. It's as simple as that.

When you try to control, you lose your connection to the universe. When you stop trying to control, alternatives surface along with an effective approach to influence the behavior you desire.

As you employ influence, you'll instantaneously feel the change in your connection to the universe. Earlier feelings of frustration and anger are replaced by a sense of well being that comes from knowing you've done all you could. Instead of frustration you'll experience deeper affection for the person and respect for their right to make their own decisions. When that happens you'll know that you are once again connected to the universe.

Let's review what the universe is telling us when as we attempt to control or influence others' behaviors.

Emotions
Control: anxiety, fear, frustration, helplessness.
Influence: care, concern, respect for others' rights to choose.

Message
Control: connection lost.
Influence: connected.

Actions

Control: shift to influence to regain connection; offer options; allow the person to choose; respect their choice.

Influence: offer options; allow the other person to choose from those options; respect the choice; hold the person accountable for his choice.

Influence is more effective than control in any situation as you'll see in the following example.

Controlling employee's behavior

A business owner lamented the fact that his employees weren't doing things in the manner he wanted. He wanted to dictate to them how they performed their tasks. If he had done that he'd have gotten the reaction the parents in the example above did—only in spades.

His employees are adults with years of experience doing their jobs. They don't take kindly to having their boss tell them that what they're doing is wrong. They'll typically respond to such a message in one of two ways. They'll either ignore his mandate or follow it to the letter...if they think it's going to fail.

Here's another example, one you've probably experienced during your career. An employee or small group of employees abuse a benefit the company provides. The company's leaders eliminate or severely restrict the benefit to stop the abuse. In the process they alienate previously happy, productive workers.

Sick days, vacation policies and golden handcuffs are all attempts to control employee behavior. These are but a few of the attempts "leaders" make to control employees' behavior. As you well know, not only do these policies fail to produce the desired result, they negatively impact employee morale. Sick-day limits pose problems for highly-skilled, highly-committed workers who are suffering severe family health issues.

Vacation policies don't consider the dedication of the most highly-productive workers or the extra hours they often put in because they are dedicated to the company's success.

Golden handcuffs often encourage retirement on the job. That's true whether employees' feel at odds with the direction the company is headed, that the job no longer challenges them, or that their new boss doesn't value their insights and input.

In situations like these, the best and brightest will leave despite golden handcuffs. The result is that the company is left trying to compete with less committed, less talented people. That's not a formula for business success.

You know from personal experience the negative emotions you experience when your company tries to control you. These are the same emotions your employees feel when you attempt to control their behavior. Negative emotions are signs from the universe that it's time to change what we're doing.

To avoid these negative emotions ask the universe "How can I accomplish [whatever your goal is] while making this a better environment for my employees?"

The universe will provide answers, often within minutes of your asking the question. Even if it takes a few days, persist in asking the question. You and your employees will reap great benefits when you reconnect with the universe.

The answer may come in the form of insights into what's working for other companies. Some of today's most successful tech companies set expectations, then allow their employees to set their own hours, determine how much vacation they'll take and when they'll take it.

The companies' expectations are lofty, but their employees are in complete control of how they meet these expectations. If they fail to meet expectations, a quick exit is assured; there are consequences for not honoring commitments.

The answer may come as a leadership approach based on influence rather than control. During my tenure in corporate America, I didn't have the ability (or wisdom) to create a policy like the one I just described. In lieu of that more enlightened policy, I had a management system that enabled direct reports to set their own goals and priorities, then held them accountable for the commitments they made. I had a three and out policy.

The first time an employee failed to complete the goals he established (assuming there wasn't a flaw in the system that prevented it) I would meet with him outside our group meeting and take responsibility for not having been clear in expressing my expectations.

If the employee failed to meet expectations the following week, we'd meet again, one on one. The difference is that this time I didn't take any responsibility for the failure. Instead, I reiterated my expectations, asked him whether he understood my expectations, then told him that if we were to meet again it would be the last meeting we would have.

I rarely fired an employee. After the second meeting the person either decided to do what he had committed to do or he left to find a position elsewhere. I was okay with either result.

Because of the candor, the clear expectations and the fact that I allowed the employee to choose whether or not he wanted to honor his commitments, I never lost my connection with the universe. I continued to enjoy my job. I knew that regardless which choice my employee made, my team and I were going to be fine. These are the benefits you gain when you stop trying to control your employees' behaviors.

These are only a couple of examples of how to deal with the control issue if you're a leader. The possibilities are endless. The approach is the same if you're an employee who is unhappy with your employment, the only thing that's different is the questions you ask.

If you're an employee who dreads going to work, feels constrained or unappreciated, ask yourself:

- What can I do to make the job more exciting and more rewarding?
- What am I doing that is contributing to the friction that exists between my boss and me?
- Am I stewing in my own dissatisfaction or candidly and respectfully communicating my concerns to my boss?
- Am I taking time to consider my boss's needs, fears, and anxiety, or am I focused solely on mine?

Only when you've explored these questions and determined that you've done what you can to improve the situation, is it appropriate to ask:

- Where can I find a job where I can grow professionally and personally?
- What will that job look like?
- What values would I expect to find in both the leaders and the people who work there?

The answers to the first set of questions will assure that you're not making an emotional decision—that you've made an effort to reconnect with the universe in your current employment.

If the first set of questions fail to produce an improvement in the enjoyment of your employment, the second set will guide you to a more enjoyable, fulfilling career.

Whether someone's trying to control you or you're trying to control someone else, the negative emotions you experience is the universe's way of telling you you're making a mistake. That's when it's time to ask the questions suggested above.

The answers the universe provides comes in many forms. It could be an article you read, an email from a friend alerting you to something he found intriguing, a news report, a book someone told you about or that you found while browsing the stacks at your local library. How it surfaces doesn't matter. The only thing that matters is that you're paying attention. The universe sends messages in many forms. It's imperative that you be continuously attuned to the messages you receive.

Let's recap what we've learned about controlling employee behaviors. Once again, it's a difference between control and influence.

Emotions
Control: anxiety, fear, frustration, helplessness.
Influence: respect, openness, excitement and encouragement.

Message
Control: connection lost.
Influence: connected.

Actions
Control: shift to influence; offer options; allow the person to choose; respect the choice; hold person accountable.

Influence: continue to elicit your employee's thoughts about alternative approaches and respect your employees' right to choose; focus on the result, not the process.

Now that you understand that the emotions you feel during attempts to control others' behavior are messages from the universe, let's see what messages the universe sends when your expectations aren't met.

Unmet expectations

"Why can't they just...?" There's hardly a day goes by that we don't ask ourselves that question. Few things frustrate us as much as not having our expectations met.

Your kids missed their bus *again*. You make an unplanned stop at the grocery store because your spouse forgot something, only to find that the store's out of what you need.

Your assistant, who repeatedly pulls your bacon from the fire, misses the deadline on the biggest proposal of your life.

Despite repeated attempts to help your daughter focus on the task at hand, you've gotten a call from her teacher saying that she's still daydreaming and still missing deadlines on her homework. On and on it goes.

When expectations aren't met, the emotions you experience range from disappointment to rage. The actions you take will dictate the results you get. To help you get the best result, let's see what the universe's messages are telling us.

Rare occurrence

If you only occasionally experience this frustration with

the person with whom you're dealing, no big deal. It happens. When it does—as soon as those words "Why can't they just...?" come to mind—remind yourself that everyone drops the ball occasionally, including you.

With this simple reminder, you'll become a more generous, forgiving person. You'll also be reminded that when you treat others this way, they're more likely to forgive your missteps. Here's an example of how people react to acts of kindness and understanding.

I arrived for a six a.m. flight after having spent two hours on the road. My expectation was that I'd be able to check in quickly and enjoy a leisurely flight. What I encountered was a long line at the check-in counter.

During my wait I noticed that everyone ahead of me railed at the young woman at the counter. When my turn came, I approached the counter saying "Wow, what a great way to start your day?"

She laughed and said "I'm sorry, but engine problems require me to schedule you on a later flight." It happens.

As she checked the seating on a nine a.m. flight, she looked up at me and said "You're pretty tall, would you like a seat near the emergency exit? The aisles are wider, you'll have more leg room." What a sweet gesture on her part.

That brief exchange highlights how it's possible to produce a wonderful outcome for all involved *when we take the time to remind ourselves that we too fail to meet others' expectations.*

Let's review the messages we're getting from the universe when, on occasion, our expectations aren't met. We can choose to see ourselves as victims or part of the solution.

Emotions

Victim: disappointed, frustrated, angry, cruel.

Solution: compassionate, empathetic, solution-orientated.

Message

Victim: connection lost.

Solution: connected.

Actions

Victim: recognize that we fail to meet others expectations; be empathetic, seek a mutually-beneficial solution.

Solution: continue to show respect and concern for others while seeking mutually-beneficial solutions.

If you rarely find yourself asking "Why can't they...?", you are doing an excellent job of setting expectations. But if this a regular occurrence you need to listen, the universe is telling you something completely different.

Frequent occurrence

If you experience disappointment, frustration or anger on a regular basis because others' aren't meeting your expectations, the universe is sending you messages. It's telling you that you are either:

- Not setting expectations.
- Not being precise in communicating what you expect.
- Not establishing consequences for failed expectations.
- Setting unreasonable expectations.

Unreasonable expectations

Let's begin with unreasonable expectations. Earlier in the book we talked about what happens when we fight our nature —when we try to force ourselves to do things we don't really want to do.

We discovered how swiftly these emotions can be replaced with feelings of joy, excitement and confidence when we stop fighting our natures. The same is true for all of us because, at the end of the day, we're all cut from the same cloth—we all possess the same human nature.

When others consistently disappoint you, it very well might be that you're asking them to fight their nature. Your natural tendency in these situations is to think that the person is "inept, lazy, doesn't care or is doing something to spite you." While these are possibilities, it's been my experience that few people are uncaring or vindictive.

When people consistently fail to meet my expectations it's often because I've asked them to do something that's contrary to their nature or their values. In doing so I've set unreasonable expectations and set us both up for disappointment.

We often see this occur in large corporations? A person is hired for the specialty he has, then he's assigned a leadership role that he's neither interested in or equipped to handle. When the person's performance fails to meet expectations, the blame falls upon him when it rightly belongs to the person who asked him to do something contrary to his nature.

We see this in personal relationships as well. Parents push their children to pursue the things without regard to whether the child likes doing them. This is especially true when the child exhibits a talent for what they're doing. As we've discussed earlier it's desire, not talent that drives success.

Spouses can feel locked into roles by virtue of their gender. Because they don't enjoy some aspect of their role, they either procrastinate or perform the task sloppily just so they finish it. Both approaches produce the same result—disappointment and frustration—because what's expected doesn't fit their nature.

Deeply-religious people want to share their joy with others. In doing so they *expect* others to embrace their beliefs and they persist in that effort. The same is true any time that we assume that our behaviors, lifestyle, beliefs and values are superior to those embraced by the other party. Expecting them to change because that's what we believe is an unreasonable expectation.

When I feel myself getting angry, frustrated or distrustful of someone because the person has repeatedly failed to meet my expectations, I know that it's time to pay attention to what the universe is telling me. The message is very similar to the message we get when we try to control the situation.

Emotions
Control: anxiety, fear, frustration, helplessness.
Influence: respect, empathy, openness, caring.

Message
Control: connection lost.
Influence: connected.

Actions
Control: shift to influence to regain connection; show your care and concern by suggesting alternatives that fit their nature, values and beliefs; be clear about your expectations; if expectations aren't likely to be met, sever the relationship respectfully recognizing each

person's right to make their own choices.

Influence: continue to show your respect for others' rights to be true to their nature, to live according to their values and beliefs, and expect them to offer you the same consideration.

If you determine that your expectation isn't unreasonable, but you're not getting the desired result, it may be that you're not setting the expectation.

No expectation set

All too often the reason my expectation isn't met is that I neglected to communicate it. As I say in *Stand Out From The Crowd*, all of us contribute to every problem we face. So if we aren't asking the person to fight his nature, it's likely we didn't set the expectation in the first place.

I'll probably get into trouble for what I'm about to say, but it's something I've observed repeatedly over the years. It's a generalization, and there are exceptions to the rule, but women tend not to communicate their expectations as readily as men.

Many women would prefer to have their expectations met without having to communicate them. That's based both on my observations and on comments from women who expressed the disappointment of unmet expectations.

When female colleagues express disappointment at not having an expectation met, I ask "Did you tell the person that's what you want?" The vast majority of the time they sheepishly reply "No, I didn't." That's true regardless of whether they're dealing with men or other women.

The reasons for this behavior, whether exhibited by men or

women, is irrelevant. What's essential to note is that you're the cause of your frustration. Let's see how the universe sends us this message.

Emotions

No expectation set: frustration, disappointment, anger.

Expectation set: clarity, confidence, mutual understanding.

Message

No expectation set: connection lost.

Expectation set: connected.

Actions

No expectation set: set expectations with the other person's input to assure congruency with their nature, values and beliefs; hold the person accountable.

Expectation set: continue to involve others' when setting expectations; hold them accountable.

If you're confident that you have set expectations and that they're reasonable (fits the person's nature), yet you aren't getting the result you desire, it may be that your communication skills could use some work.

Imprecise language

Men have their foibles as well. While men may be more inclined to communicate their expectations, they often aren't precise in their language or they demand rather than request. Neither produces a favorable result.

Regardless of your gender, when you're not using precise language you leave your expectation open to interpretation. In situations like this, the odds are against you. You're not likely to get what you want. When you set an expectation and the other person provides something other than what you expected ask yourself "How could I have expressed my wishes more clearly?" Remember, your subconscious mind responds well to the *how* questions.

One of the pieces of information that is most often missing in communicating expectations is a deadline. You've had this happen to you. You get a request from your boss. He doesn't indicate a deadline so you set the project aside so that you can finish what you're doing.

A couple of hours later your boss comes in to check on the progress of your assignment. Both of you become frustrated and bitter by the the urgency the poor communication creates.

On the flip side, when we're the ones who fail to set deadlines, if we're honest with ourselves about our mistake, we feel stupid, embarrassed and sympathetic to the people our mistake inconvenienced.

We open the door for a similar result when every request we make is urgent. This practice invites people to discount the urgency and, in doing so, opens the door to missed deadlines.

Here's how imprecise language manifests itself:

Emotions
Imprecise: disappointment, frustration, anxiety, anger.
Precise: success, joy, confidence, appreciation.

Message

Imprecise: connection lost.

Precise: connected.

Actions

Imprecise: before making a request take a few minutes to assure that you're communicating all of your expectations including deadlines.

Precise: continue whatever practices you're employing; you are consistently getting what you expect.

Tone

Another reason why your expectation isn't being met might be the tone of your expectation. In *Stand Out From The Crowd* we discussed the fact that no one likes to be told what to do—in fact, our natural tendency is to resist being told anything.

With that in mind when your expectations aren't being met, you know you haven't asked the person to fight his nature, and you've set expectations with precise language, then explore the possibility that your tone created resistance. Requests elicit the help you desire, demands don't.

The universe let's you know whether you're using the right tone by the other person's reaction. Here's what you'll see:

Emotions

Demand: resentment, resistance, defiance.

Request: respect, interest, engagement, a desire to please.

Message

Demand: connection lost.

Request: connected.

Actions

Demand: apologize for having made a demand, show your appreciation for how well the person consistently performs, engage them in developing a reasonable expectation.

Request: continue what you're doing; it's respectful, open, engaging and appreciative.

If you've met all of the above conditions and you're still not getting your expectations met, it's probably because there are no consequences.

Consequences

It's essential that there be consequences when expectations aren't met. We human beings tend not to do things that are in our best interest *unless there are consequences for not doing so.*

A child who fails to clean his room at the time and in the manner agreed upon will not learn responsibility unless there are consequences for failing to honor his commitment. This was never more evident than in a recent experience I had as a college professor.

Out of a class of 37 students, five failed to meet the final exam deadline *despite the fact that the syllabus and repeated reminders during class clearly that I would NOT accept late submissions.* Since the final exam represented 40% of their grade, all five failed the course.

I'm convinced that had they experienced consequences for their actions when they were younger, they wouldn't have been so cavalier in their approach to deadline.

Today's best run companies set performance expectations,

but leave the method for meeting expectations to the employee. An employee's repeated failure to meet expectations results in quick termination of their employment...as it should.

Here's how the universe let's you know that you're not holding others accountable for what they've agreed to do:

Emotions

No consequences: disappointment, frustration, anger.
Consequences: peace of mind; free of guilt and anxiety.

Message

No consequences: connection lost.
Consequences: connected.

Actions

No consequences: engage the other party in establishing the consequences for their actions; hold the person accountable.

Consequences: enjoy the peace of mind that comes when you've involved the other party in setting expectations and consequences; recognize that their failure to meet expectations was their choice—a choice to which they are entitled.

Now that we've explored the daily-living experience of unmet expectations, let's turn our attention to the seemingly unlikely source of frustration—giving.

Giving

Typically when we give we experience joy. We feel good about ourselves. It's the psychic reward the universe affords.

There are, however, times when giving becomes a source of frustration and resentment. There are a couple of reasons for this:

1. Your motivation for giving is misguided.
2. You feel that you're being taken for granted.

Wrong motivation

The first occurs when we give with an expectation that the other party will reciprocate. This is as true in business as it is in our personal lives.

In business this is the complaint I hear most often: "I gave [name] x number of referrals that generated y dollars of revenue for him, but have never gotten a referral in return."

Similar complaints are heard in dealings of a more personal nature. The person gives expecting that the other person will do something nice in return. When it doesn't happen, bitterness ensues and relationships falter. It doesn't have to be that way.

The late Jim Rohn, entrepreneur and inspirational speaker, said that none of us gives magnanimously—that human beings aren't wired that way. He went on to say that the enlightened among us give without an expectation of getting anything back from the person to whom we're giving. Instead they know that the universe will repay them in some way in the future.

I couldn't agree more. I have never been able to get ahead of the giving curve. No matter how much I give, the universe returns multiples of what I've given.

Those who haven't achieved "enlightenment" don't realize that when you give expecting something in return, you move whatever you're giving out of the realm of a gift to that of a trade—an exchange.

It's no longer a gift, it's a transaction. As a result the "gift" not only loses it's generous nature, it often creates resentment on the part of the recipient who senses an expectation that isn't being communicated.

Another possible outcome is that the recipient, not realizing that the giver expects something in return, presumes that gift is a gift. Later the recipient wonders why the giver's generosity suddenly stops and there's tension when they meet.

Sound familiar? It's another form of unmet expectations resulting from poor communication. The moral of the story is don't give unless you intend whatever you're giving to be a gift. If you want something in exchange for what you're giving make that clear up front.

Here's a comparison of what you experience when you give with and without expectation.

Emotions

Trade: disappointment, resentment, separation.

Gift: joy, gratitude for the good fortune you possess, generosity, a rewarding connection with the other person and the universe.

Message

Trade: connection lost.

Gift: connected.

Actions

Trade: recall the good things that have come your way and recognize them as gifts from the universe; share your gifts with others knowing that the universe rewards you with multiples of what you give.

Gift: continue what you're doing; your generosity makes the world a better place.

Taken for granted

The other source of frustration in giving occurs when you are *repeatedly* asked for help by someone without any sense that they appreciate what you're doing for them or that they care about you other than for what you can do for them.

While you should always give as Mr. Rohn suggests, there are people who would, if you allow them to, take advantage of your generous nature.

In these situations, it's alright to stop giving. You have a right to respect. Someone who regularly takes advantage of you isn't respecting you. There are some simple, respectful ways of communicating the fact that you're no longer going to allow the other person to take advantage of your good nature.

In business I simply say "That's what people pay me for." It sends the message without denigrating the other person.

My friend, Larry Lukens, a very successful salesperson, expresses it this way. When a business owner, who repeatedly benefited from Larry's advice without ever buying from him asked for more advice Larry asked, "Would you plant your seed in a field that doesn't produce?" The business owner said no. Larry responded "Nor do I." That ended the request.

The same approach works in personal relationships. You

should not allow family and friends to take advantage of your good nature. You can communicate the fact that you're no longer going to be the answer to their problems. Simply say "I didn't mind helping you out earlier, but it's time for you to take control of the situation so that the problem doesn't persist."

Using this approach you're not only communicating your unwillingness to be taken for granted, you're letting the person know that you're not going to enable behaviors that don't serve them well.

You should not allow anyone to take advantage of your generous nature, but when drawing a line in the sand you need to be respectful as you communicate that fact.

Emotions

Patsy: frustration, resentment, irritation, avoidance.

Dignity: confidence, self-respect, power, self-worth.

Message

Patsy: connection lost.

Dignity: connected.

Actions

Patsy: realize that if you want others to respect you, you have to respect yourself; that includes saying "no" to people who would take advantage of your generous nature.

Dignity: continue to give generously; the universe rewards you with multiples of whatever you give; when others abuse your good nature, deny future requests from them using language that's respectful, yet clear.

Now let's turn our attention to what it means when we feel like we're victims.

Victim

Who among us hasn't at one time or another asked "Why me?" It's in these moments that we feel like we're victims—that God or the universe has abandoned us.

The reality is that everyone has challenges in their lives; no one is exempt. When I saw athletes enjoy great financial and career success, I mistakenly assumed that they were leading privileged lives. Then I'd see a news story indicating that they had a child with Asperger or Down's syndrome, or that they'd lost a loved one in a tragic accident.

I realized that no one gets a pass when it comes to pain and suffering. Yet these amazing people continue to excel at what they do while dealing with the same challenges you and I do. What makes the difference?

I believe that there are three things that account for their success. They:

1. Have a desire to succeed that won't be denied.
2. Take the action needed to assure their success.
3. Are grateful for the success they've enjoyed.

We've already discussed the roles desire and action play. I won't bore you by repeating them here. Gratitude is something we haven't discussed. It's importance can't be overstated. It's the key to resilience—to setting aside the *why me* question.

My dear friend, Cathy Sexton, and her family have suffered more health issues and losses of family members than any three families I know. Yet, Cathy's spirit is as indomitable as the athletes I mentioned above.

When asked how she can continue to remain upbeat and selfless in the face of all the adversity she's faced she says "It's gratitude. Everyday I remind myself of the wonderful family and friends I have, of the fact that I get to do what I truly enjoy, that my friends are always there for me when I need them."

The next time you wonder "Why me?" recognize it for what it is—a reminder from the universe that you need to be grateful for all the good things in your life.

Joseph Addison put it this way, "A contented mind is the greatest blessing a man can enjoy in this world." Alfred Nobel echoed this sentiment when he said "Contentment is the only real wealth." In a more humorous fashion Winston Churchill said "If you feel like you're going through hell, keep moving."

At the end of the day whether or not you feel like a victim boils down to gratitude. When you're grateful for all the good things in your life, it's much easier to sustain the desire and action needed to achieve whatever you choose in life.

Start your day recalling the riches you enjoy. The Addison quote is on a tapestry that hangs just inside my bedroom door. It's the first thing I see as I begin a new day. That simple quote reminds me of all that makes life wonderful while fueling my desire to pursue any goal that intrigues me. It's the best of all possible worlds—contentment and desire. It's easier to move forward when you're happy. Gratitude fuels happiness.

Let's recap what the universe is telling you when you feel like a victim.

Emotions
Victim: alone, helpless, frustrated, angry, envious.
Grateful: happy, confident, energized, capable of coping with anything you face.

Message
Victim: connection lost.
Grateful: connected.

Actions
Victim: shift your focus to all the good that exists in your life; be grateful for that good; commit yourself to using the good to help others—for it's in helping others that we help ourselves.

Grateful: continue to begin each day with reminders of all the good that exists in your life; realize that contentment and gratitude don't preclude desire, they enhance desire; pursue whatever you want in life with vigor, it gives you more reasons to be grateful.

It's time to shift our focus to another source of frustration—relationship problems. Who doesn't have those?

Annoying personalities

The vast majority of people we meet are pleasant, likable folks. Some even endear themselves so quickly that they warm our hearts and inspire us to greater kindness. Occasionally we meet someone whose presence elicits dread and an avoidance response. Once again, these emotions are messages from the universe. Let's see what they're telling us.

These feelings indicate that we're:

1. Making judgments made upon first impressions.
2. Ignoring the fact that others tolerate our idiosyncrasies.
3. Overlooking the unique value others possess.

Let's take a look at each of these in more detail.

First impressions

Abraham Lincoln offered a good approach to dealing with negative first impressions when he said "I don't like that man. I must get to know him better."

Lincoln understood that everyone:

- Has value.
- Brings something worthwhile to the table.
- Judges based on first impressions.
- Loses when those first impressions override the ability to really get to know the person.

Armed with this awareness, Lincoln committed himself to looking beyond annoying aspects of the person's personality to the value the person possessed.

Our idiosyncrasies

The avoidance reaction we experience when we meet an annoying personality is the universe's way of reminding us that others find some of our behaviors and attitudes equally trying.

When others are kind enough to point them out to us, they open the door to richer, more rewarding personal relationships for us.

I'm sure some of you are cringing at the prospect of having someone point our your eccentricities, even more so when you consider the possibility of confronting others with theirs. These are natural, albeit misguided, feelings.

The good news is that helping others overcome annoying behaviors doesn't have to be confrontational or denigrating. The key is to frame your message as a desire to help them. It also helps to point out how someone made you aware of something you were doing that caused you problems and how much you appreciated the person's kindness. If, after employing this approach, the person exhibits resentment or resistance, that's their problem not yours. You've done what you can to help the person, they're not open to receiving help.

To illustrate the point that others appreciate candor, I'll share a personal experience with you. I was in the process of firing a client because she wasn't doing what I suggested and, as a result, wasn't going to get a return on her investment with me. When I finished explaining this to her she said "Dale, you are telling me this and what I feel is love."

I was firing her as a client and yet she realized that in doing so I was looking out for her best interests. That's why she was feeling love. You have the ability to produce similar results.

The key is to frame what you're about to say in terms of how it helps the other person. That way there's no judgment involved, no denigration of the other person, simply an act of kindness that'll help the person enjoy greater success in future relationships.

When you frame your message in these terms, you'll find the other person is very appreciative. Even better, it's highly likely that you'll make a friend for life. That's a win worth pursuing!

Another way that I know that people appreciate candor is when they look me squarely in the eye and say "Dale, I don't always agree with you, but I always know where I stand with you."

Implicit in this statement is both an indication of mutual respect and an appreciation for my candor in dealing with them. These feelings of respect and appreciation open the door to the third aspect of the universe's annoying-personality message— that we're missing out on the value others possess.

Missing out

I'm certain that you've met some brilliant people who have some really annoying habits. You've probably thought "If only they didn't..., they'd enjoy so much more success."

When you avoid someone who possesses annoying habits, you deprive yourself of the value they possess. You also limit the number of people who would be willing to help you when you need it. These are high prices to pay for being unwilling to overlook their annoying habits.

Instead of alienating the person by avoiding them (something they sense as readily as you do when someone avoids you), take a few moments to look past whatever it is that repels you and, as Lincoln suggests, get to know the person better.

Better yet, as you get to know them, tell them how they can enjoy greater success by changing an annoying habit into one that's attractive. You'll create a life-long friend.

Before we move on, let's revisit the messages the universe is sending when we encounter annoying personalities.

Emotions

Avoidance:	annoyance, resistance, embarrassment, guilt.
Acceptance:	care, empathy, kindness, self-awareness.

Message

Avoidance:	connection lost.
Acceptance:	connected.

Actions

Avoidance:	remind yourself that you too have behaviors that others find annoying; recall their tolerance; extend that consideration to others; alert them to more productive behaviors.
Acceptance:	acceptance is wonderful, assistance priceless; help others to replace annoying behaviors with those that will enhance their relationships with others.

You know what it's like to feel overwhelmed. Let's see what the universe is telling us when this feeling surfaces.

Overwhelmed

It's rare that a day goes by without someone telling me that they feel overwhelmed, stressed and generally miserable. What I've observed is that people who feel overwhelmed exhibit one of the following three characteristics. They are:

- Pleasers.
- Overly-optimistic.
- Lack a systematic approach.

Let's explore each of these characteristics in more detail.

Pleasers

There are people among us who love helping others—so much so that they can't say "no" to any request they receive. I've seen business people with this tendency give away so much information in the sales call that they lose the sale.

Parents who want their children to have an opportunity to try enjoy a plethora of experiences, run themselves, and their kids, ragged instead of making conscious choices about what's in their and their kids' best interests.

Some people ignore their own well-being to please others —a habit that can have serious health consequences.

Regardless of the motivation, "no" is not part of these folks vocabulary. If you're one of them, here are some tips for you.

- Acknowledge the fact that you enjoy helping others; it's a good thing.
- Be honest with yourself about the toll it's taking on you.
- Ask the universe how you can help others in a way that benefits both them and you.
- Employ the answer the universe provides.

NOTE: These are simple concepts, but because of your natural tendency, overcoming them will require:

- Constant monitoring of your desire to help.
- Awareness of the cost you incur when you say "yes."
- The ability to say "no" when the cost is high.
- Paying attention to the universe's messages.

The first step is to quickly recognize negative feelings for what they are—messages from the universe.

The second step is to interpret the message accurately. If you're a pleaser that means acknowledging that you're forgoing your interests in pursuit of the gratification you gain when you help others.

During this second step, your natural tendency will be to try to understand what motivates you to place others' interests ahead of your own. Don't! You'll waste time and delay your connection to the universe. As noted psychotherapist, David Reynolds, said in his book, *Playing Ball in Running Water*, the primary difference between psychotherapy in the East (Japan) and that in the United States is that therapists in the East don't worry about why people behave as they do, they simply help them develop better habits.

That's the approach you should use. The Eastern approach will accelerate your adoption of new, more beneficial behaviors while freeing you of the guilt and self-deprecation associated with trying to discover your motivation.

The third step in the process should be the one in which you decide what you're going to do when you get a request. The best thing to do is to pause and buy yourself some time to make an informed decision. The simplest way to buy time is to tell the person "I'll have to check my calendar."

People understand that we all have time constraints—that we're all busy and often have more things on our plate than we can handle. They'll accept the fact that you need to check your availability.

When you're no longer in the person's presence, use the following process to help you make an informed decision:

- Ask yourself "Is this something I really *want* to do or is it something I feel *compelled* to do?"
- If it's not something you want to do, tell the person no. And do it quickly, otherwise you'll fret over whether or not you're making the right decision and exhaust yourself in the process.
- If it is something you want to do ask yourself "Based on what I've already committed to doing, where does this request rank in terms of interest to me?"
- If it ranks lower than the items to which you've already committed, tell the person no. Again, do it quickly.
- If it holds greater interest than some of the earlier commitments you've made, ask yourself "Can that earlier commitment be postponed without damaging the people to whom the commitment was made?"
- If the answer is yes, make sure that postponing the earlier commitment won't create a problem for others. Then agree to the new request.
- If the earlier commitment can't be postponed without damaging others, then say no to the current request. Then promise yourself that you'll use this process to avoid missing out on something in the future because you've overcommitted.
- Finally, build a half hour or hour into your schedule each day for "you" time. This is time that you can use to accept a request that intrigues you or to have time to simply allow your mind to wander. You'll be amazed at the insights and ideas you gain during this quiet time.

The key to the success of this process is understanding that you don't fail people when you say no. You fail them when you say yes, but don't follow through. Telling them no enables them to find alternative ways of getting what they need.

This approach also helps parents who strive to give their children every opportunity possible. It gives them the tools to teach their children how to manage commitments so that they don't feel overwhelmed? Is it ever too early for them to learn this lesson?

Ask yourself "Do I really want my children to experience the stress and anxiety I feel because I'm overwhelmed?" If not, it's imperative that you make better choices for yourself and your children. Remember that children mimic their parents' behavior. When you consistently make good choices, they do as well.

One more thought for all of you. When you overcommit then drop the ball, you not only damage the party, you damage your reputation as well. Pleasers, people who desperately want to be viewed as kind, generous, and helpful, are instead viewed as kindhearted, but unreliable. Ouch!

You can avoid earning this reputation, and having others take advantage of your kind nature, by pausing to consider the request and its impact on you before deciding. During this pause, you can also consider whether the person making the request is someone who has a history of taking advantage of your generous nature.

As Jim Rohn suggested, you don't want to give with an expectation of getting something in return from the person to whom you're giving. At the same time I don't believe in giving consistently to people whose only interests are their own—who are takers who have little, if any, interest in your welfare.

If you're not a pleaser, or a parent who's trying too hard to expose your child to the vast array of opportunities that exist, you may be overly-optimistic about what you can accomplish.

Overly-optimistic

Actually there are two possibilities here: (1) you're truly overly-optimistic, (2) you enjoy what you do.

We'll begin with the second possibility. I'm certain you've had this experience.

It's late afternoon on a work day. You know that you won't be able to complete the next item on your "to do" list before day's end. You scan your list and find something you know that you can complete before you leave.

Be honest. How often do you complete that task *before* day's end? My experience is that I rarely completed the task that day. It almost always carried over to the next day. Why?

It's our perception of time. When we do things we don't enjoy, time seems to pass at an excruciatingly slow pace. Even simple tasks seen to take forever to complete.

Conversely, when we're doing things we enjoy time seems to fly. We find ourselves amazed at the fact that hours passed without our realizing it.

This awareness will help you more effectively interpret the universe's messages. When you get frustrated because things take longer than you expect, it's because you're:

- Overly optimistic.
- Not enjoying the task.

If you're not enjoying the task, send a message to your subconscious mind that the next time a similar task surfaces, you're going to delegate the task, or hire someone to do it for you. You'll not only get better results, you'll maintain your connection to the universe.

If you enjoy the task, but consistently underestimate the time needed to complete it, track your time. Then store that information in your subconscious mind for future reference. What you'll find is that the next time you face that task, your subconscious mind will remind you that it takes x amount of time to complete the task. The universe, via your subconscious mind, helps you avoid the stress and frustration you previously experienced.

Another reason for feeling overwhelmed is that you lack a systematic approach to what you do.

No system

Imagine for a moment that you have no memory—none at all. That means that every time you embark on an activity it's as if you've never performed the task before. The inefficiency inherent in that scenario is mind-boggling. Yet that's precisely what some of us *choose* to do.

We make excuses for our behavior saying things like:

- What I do is unique.
- Every situation is different.
- I don't have time to plan.
- Nothing goes according to plan.

The reality is that these excuses are designed to mask our reluctance to develop systems for dealing with the tasks we perform. Yet the most efficient and least stressed among us all employ systems.

We often lament the fact that others are able to accomplish so much more than we can—that they enjoy greater success *and* more free time than we do. The reason is that they have systematic approaches to what they do.

If you're experiencing feelings of being overwhelmed and you realize that it's because you don't have a system, you have two choices. You can:

1. Continue to live with the stress you're experiencing.
2. Develop systems to alleviate that stress.

If you choose to continue your current practices, make the choice consciously so that you can be happy with that choice. I know very bright people who are happiest when they're riding the cusp between busy and overwhelmed.

However, if you choose to become more systematic, ask your subconscious *how* you can do so. It'll provide an answer that is consistent with your nature. The system it provides will be just enough to dramatically reduce the stress of feeling overwhelmed while allowing you the flexibility that you desire.

Here's an example to illustrate how the universe aligns its suggestions to your nature. My dear friend and founder of On Target For Profitable Growth, Lori St. Clair, and I presented a program on planning. Her natural style is to gather and analyze as much relevant information as possible before establishing her plan. As you might suspect, her plan is highly detailed.

I am Lori's polar opposite. When something intrigues me, I identify the first few steps I need to take (a general direction in which I need to go) and I start moving. What I learn from these initial steps determines what I do next. That's my "plan."

What Lori and I find interesting is that, despite our starkly contrasting approaches to planning, we both knew when we had enough information to proceed. When we reached that point, we stopped gathering data, established a plan, and took the initial steps.

We did so while experiencing precisely the same emotions —freedom from doubt, fear and anxiety. We were excited and energized by the possibilities and able to move forward quickly and confidently. It's in moments like these that you feel your connection to the universe.

Before we move onto our next daily living experience, let's recap what we've learned about feeling overwhelmed.

Emotions

Overwhelmed: stressed, exhausted, irritable, anxious, guilty.

In control: joyful, efficient, powerful, energetic, valued.

Message

Overwhelmed: connection lost.

In control: connected.

Actions

Overwhelmed: determine whether you're a pleaser, overly-optimistic, or lack a systematic approach; employ the tips outlined above to regain and maintain your connection.

In control: continue to employ the practices that enable you to enjoy your connection to the universe; employ whatever suggestions above will help you solidify and enhance the enjoyment of your connection.

Do you procrastinate when you feel that what you need to do is going to create a problem or ill will? Let's find out what these feelings really mean—what the universe is really telling us about that situation.

Inflated problems

At times we postpone things we know we should be doing because we anticipate problems. This is particularly true when we know that we need to have a conversation that we believe may become confrontational. Here's an example.

A client kept postponing conversations with his earliest customers over the need for a price increase. He had raised prices on new customers and some longer-term customers without incident. Yet he was resisting having the conversation with his earliest customers. When I asked why, he said it was because he felt indebted to them for the confidence and trust they'd placed in him when he was getting started. He liked these people and didn't want to lose them as clients.

He agreed that he needed to have the conversation, but kept postponing the conversation saying "It's a big thing." I asked "Is it really a big thing or are you making it a big thing?"

After reflecting on the question, he acknowledged that it wasn't any bigger conversation than those he'd had with other customers—that he was making it bigger than it needed to be.

He also realized that his other customers had seen the value of his services and readily accepted the price increase. There was no reason to expect that his earliest customers would react differently. Indeed, his earliest customers had more reasons to pay a higher price. They'd been benefitting from his advice for a longer period of time.

Whenever you're resisting a conversation or failing to take action because you fear that it's a "big thing," remember that you're feeding that emotion into your subconscious mind and, consequently the universe, where doubts, fears and anxiety are nurtured.

Stop resisting something you need to do. Instead ask your subconscious, "*How* can I accomplish [result] while respecting the other person's needs?" The solution the universe suggests will be simple and effective.

Armed with this solution, you'll feel confident that you can be successful. Confidence replaces the fear and anxiety you're experiencing. You'll take action quickly, decisively, with great respect and concern for the welfare of the other party. That's a winning combination!

Not convinced? Let me ask you "How often have you had a conversation that you expected to be difficult only to find that it wasn't nearly as bad as you expected?" "Almost always" is the answer I get most often. I'll bet it was your answer as well.

Let's take a look at the difference in feelings we experience when we inflate problems instead of viewing them realistically.

Emotions
Inflated: anxious, fearful, torn, stymied.
Realistic: confident, caring, resolved, proactive.

Message
Inflated: connection lost.
Realistic: connected.

Actions

Inflated: remind yourself that your inflating the problem; ask the universe how you can take the action, or have the conversation, while producing a good result for both parties.

Realistic: continue to ask the universe *how* to demonstrate care and concern for others *even when taking actions or delivering messages they may not like.*

Now that you have ways of dealing with procrastination, let's explore the frustration we, at times, experience at others' good fortune.

Envy

You don't have to feel like a victim to feel resentment or envy over the good fortune others experience. It's a natural, albeit futile, reaction to others' success.

These feelings of resentment or envy are messages from the universe telling us that we're looking at others' success inappropriately. Indeed, we're looking solely at their good fortune, not at what they did to experience that success.

While it's natural to view others' good fortune as luck, this attitude presumes the universe favors some people over others. Believing that is an indication that you may possess a victim's mindset. If so, revisit the victim section above.

If, however, you see the folly in this presumption, you have the wherewithal to put a stop to the envy you're experiencing.

My experience has been that the success any of us enjoys is the byproduct of desire and action. Those who enjoy greater success possess a greater desire for success than others in their field and, as a result, take action more quickly and consistently than their counterparts.

If you're attributing others' success to luck, if you resent or envy others' success, the universe is telling you that it's time to evaluate your desire for success and your willingness to take action. See chapters 4 and 3 respectively.

If you're unwilling to go through this evaluation process, your actions indicate that you don't really want what you say you want. If you did, you would take the action necessary to evaluate your desire and willingness to take action.

Let's summarize what we've learned about envy.

Emotions

Envy: resentment over being treated unfairly, a victim.

Joy: happy, inspired, excited, energized, grateful.

Message

Envy: connection lost.

Joy: connected.

Actions

Envy: rid yourself of the misperception that people are "lucky;" examine what they did that enabled them to enjoy the success they achieved; no one enjoys success without effort, even lottery winners wait in line to buy tickets.

Joy: continue to celebrate others' success, it elevates you and them; use others' success to inspire and sustain you during your periods of doubt; regularly remind yourself that nothing worthwhile is achieved without consistent, persistent effort.

Speaking of persistent, there are few things more annoying than persistent problems. Let's see what message the universe is sending when we experience persistent problems.

Persistent problems

When problems persistent, our natural tendency is to lay the blame on others or the system. My experience is that it's the universe telling me that *I* need to reexamine what *I'm* doing that contributes to the problem.

I delve into this in greater detail in *Stand Out From The Crowd*, but it's worth mentioning here as well. We contribute to every problem we face. When there is a problem, all parties involved own a portion of the blame. Yet the only behavior we can control is our own.

When I look first at my contribution to the problem, I not only find a simple, inexpensive, easily-implemented solution, I discover precisely what I need to do to avoid experiencing that problem again in the future. Here are a couple of examples to illustrate my point.

Micro-managing boss

My temper would flare every time my boss would come into my office to check on the progress I was making on a task he'd given me. I had the attitude of "give me the ball, get out of my way, and you'll be delighted with the result."

What I failed to realize is that my failure to communicate created anxiety for the boss. He didn't know whether I was making progress or had completely forgotten the assignment.

Once I realized what I was doing, I would take 30 seconds

a couple of times a week to let my boss know what was going on. The reason my "problem" persisted is that I wasn't looking at my contribution to the problem. Once I did, the problem was easily resolved.

Learning styles

My wife is a visual learner. I'm an auditory learner. That means that I learn best from listening while my wife learns best from visual representations.

When I get frustrated while trying to "explain" things to her, it's the universe telling me "Dummy, that's not how she prefers to learn. You need to create a visual so that she can 'see' what you're saying."

My wife's not the problem. It's my failure to recognize her natural learning style that creates the frustration I experience. As soon as I recognize this message from the universe and shift to a visual presentation, "problem" solved.

As I said, I contribute to every problem I face. This is just one more example of that fact. When a problem persists, it's because I'm not paying attention to what the universe is telling me.

Here's another example of how we are misinterpreting the universe's message when problems persist.

Different manifestations

I have the good fortune to develop close relationships with my clients. As a result they share their personal as well as business challenges with me. One of the things I've noticed is that the ones who complain the their employees aren't performing to expectations are the same people who bemoan the fact that their kids don't listen to them.

These people fail to realize that both their business and personal experiences are messages from the universe indicating that they're not holding people accountable for their actions. They're either failing to establish consequences or failing to enforce the consequences.

They have precisely the same problems persisting in two different venues that are actually the same problem. By all means when you're experiencing a problem in one area of you life, explore the possibility that other persistent problems you face are simply different manifestations of the same problem.

The next time a problem persists, take a few seconds to ask your subconscious mind:

- How am I contributing to this problem?
- What can I do to solve this problem?
- How can I avoid this problem in the future?

You'll notice that these are *how* type questions—the kind that your subconscious mind is designed to handle. Here's what you experience depending on the approach you use in dealing with persistent problems.

Emotions

Recurring: frustrated, angry, inept, helpless.
Infrequent: capable, confident, creative, empowered.

Message

Recurring: connection lost.
Infrequent: connected.

Actions

Recurring:	look for your contribution to the problem; ask for a solution to the problem; ask for guidance on how to avoid the problem in the future.
Infrequent:	you're doing a good job of looking beyond the problem to ways to avoid it in the future; keep it up.

Now that you know what it means when you get frustrated by persistent problems, let's see what it means when the source of that frustration comes from not being heard or recognized.

Not valued

There are few things more frustrating than the feeling that our opinions aren't valued or that we're not being recognized for the good we do.

While we tend to blame others for "not giving our ideas a fair hearing" or for "failing to acknowledge our skills, wisdom, or the results we've produced," the universe is telling us is that we're doing something that's preventing us from getting the recognition we desire.

The most common mistakes we make are:

- Seeking recognition.
- Being imprecise in our language.
- Offering unsolicited advice.

Let's explore each of these in more detail.

Seeking recognition

You know people who seek recognition over results. How do you react to them? Do you feel inclined to help them? Or secretly hope that their attempts to get recognized fail?

Personally I'm ill-inclined to help people whose primary goal is to get recognized. I prefer to work with those who want to do things that enrich others' lives and could care less about whether they're recognized for their efforts. As the following example will illustrate, I believe that the desire for recognition is as detrimental to the person seeking recognition as it is to those around them.

I've often thought that Carly Fiorina's brief tenure at HP (Hewlett Packard) was due in part to her desire for recognition. If you recall, shortly after becoming HP's CEO Ms. Fiorina appeared in every television ad the company produced. She set herself up as the face of HP.

There's no question that Ms. Fiorina is an extremely bright, talented woman. However, HP was founded on and thrived upon collaboration. HP's founders, despite the organization's phenomenal success, were rarely in the news and when they were, attributed the company's success to their employees.

Imagine that you were an employee of HP at the time Ms. Fiorina took the helm. Prior to her arrival you, as a member of an amazingly creative team, were enjoying great success and basking in the admiration of those who wished they could be a part of the team.

Immediately following Ms. Fiorina's arrival, she became the focal point of all the ads HP ran. Little, if anything, was said in the ads about the amazing people like you who were driving innovation.

How would you feel? Would you want to contribute to Ms.

Fiorina's success? I'm not suggesting that anyone deliberately sabotaged Ms. Fiorina's success. I don't believe that happened. Yet, you and I know how quickly our performance wanes when we're working for someone we don't like.

I take no pride in admitting that when I wasn't happy with an employment, I felt myself becoming lackadaisical in my work. Fortunately I quickly recognized what was happening and sought other employment. I knew how quickly my skills and abilities would deteriorate if I didn't extricate myself from that toxic situation.

This awareness of how people respond to self-promotion is essential in getting others to value your opinion—to gaining the recognition you deserve.

If you're feeling frustrated because you're not getting "a fair hearing" or not "being recognized for what you do," check your motivation. If your time is spent trying to get recognized instead of producing results, you've found the source of your problem.

Let's turn to the second reason why you may not be getting the recognition you desire—imprecise language.

Imprecise language

When you find people tuning you out it's typically for one of two reasons. Either you're:

1. Not being precise in your language.
2. Or being verbose.

The former initially results in requests for clarification. As questions mount you lose listeners' interest and confidence.

When that happens they tune you out.

Verbosity produces a similar result. The longer it takes you to make your point, or the more that you belabor your point, the more impatient listeners become. Their impatience grows, their attention wanes.

In both cases, you get the feeling that your thoughts and ideas aren't valued—that you can never get a fair hearing for what you have to say.

In these situations, the anger and frustration you experience is the universe telling you that you need to find a better way of communicating. Here are a couple of tips:

- Take note of the clarifying questions you're getting; they hold the key to becoming more precise in your language.
- When you're losing the listener's interest, ask yourself whether you're taking too long to make the point or belaboring the point.

Something that's served me well over the years is mentally replaying conversations I have. An hour-long meeting can be reviewed within a matter of a few minutes.

While replaying your meeting pay particular attention to the times when you lost the listener's interest. Ask yourself "What did I say that caused the person to lose interest? What language can I use to avoid losing their interest in the future?"

Also pay attention to the times when you generated interest and excitement. Make note of the language you used so that you can use it again in the future. This simple technique will help you become more precise in your language.

Now let's turn our attention to the third explanation for why we aren't getting the hearing or recognition we desire—offering unsolicited advice.

Unsolicited advice

There are few things that we resent more than unsolicited advice. It doesn't matter how sage that advice is. If it's not wanted, it's resented and ignored.

When we feel our advice isn't being heeded, our natural tendency is to push harder—to become more emphatic and insistent in promoting our ideas.

What we fail to realize, often until it's too late, is that the harder we push, the greater the resistance we create. If you feel that your message isn't being heard, one of the things that the universe is suggesting is that you may be offering advice where it isn't wanted.

A person, who says he wants to lose weight, but doesn't exercise or change his eating habits, isn't likely to want, or act upon, your suggestions that he do so.

One of the questions to ask yourself when you are angry because you're not being heard is "Am I offering unsolicited advice?" As with all of the questions posed in these examples, the answers help you regain your connection to the universe.

Let's review what the messages the universe sends when we're aren't feeling valued.

Emotions

Ignored:　　　frustrated, angry, undervalued, unappreciated.
Recognized:　 valued, confident, creative, caring, helpful.

Message

Ignored: connection lost.

Recognized: connected.

Actions

Ignored: look for the source of your frustration; is your primary goal recognition, are you imprecise in your language or offering unsolicited advice?

Recognized: keep doing what you're doing while striving to become even more precise in your language and more consistent in recognizing others for the value they provide.

As I indicated at the beginning of this chapter, I can't cover all of the situations you face on a daily basis. Those that I have covered represent the ones I see most frequently—the ones that disconnect us from the universe and, consequently, become the source of anxiety, fear, frustration and all the other negative emotions we experience.

My goal in this chapter was to help you understand both the source of your distress and share tips for regaining your connection to the universe. What I'd really like is for you to *avoid* the distress by maintaining your connection throughout the day, everyday. That's the focus of the next chapter.

CHAPTER 8
Enjoying your connection

Maintenance is cheaper than repair.—Charles Furtwengler

My dad was an automotive mechanic at the Ford dealer in my home town. He regularly reminded me, and my brothers, that maintenance is *always* cheaper than repairs.

That's as true for your connection to the universe as it is to maintaining your automobile. It's much easier to maintain your connection to the universe than to regain it.

While that may seem obvious, let's see how much energy is really needed to maintain a connection versus regaining it.

Maintaining a connection
1. Taking a few seconds at the beginning of the day to remind your subconscious mind that you want to be connected to the universe throughout the day.

Regaining a connection
1. Experience negative emotions.
2. Recognize that they're messages from the universe.
3. Ask the universe how you can regain your connection.
4. Recognize the universe's response.
5. Implement the universe's suggestion.

94

It's obvious which of these two approaches:

- Requires less energy.
- Increases your productivity.
- Enables you to *consistently* experience feelings of joy, peace and fulfillment.

Here are the keys to enjoying a connection to the universe throughout the day *everyday*:

1. Your subconscious mind is your connection.
2. You strengthen your connection in the service of others.
3. Tap into your subconscious throughout the day.

I've taken the liberty of providing a daily routine that will streamline the process to the point that you're only spending a few minutes at the beginning of each day to enjoy a connection throughout the day.

Daily routine
At the beginning of the day:

Be grateful
At the beginning of each day remind yourself the good that exists in your life, especially when you experience challenges over which you have little control—health issues, a death in the family, a lost job, financial setbacks. By recalling the good in your life you avoid feeling like a victim.

Serve others

Make the following commitment each and everyday:

I will leave everyone I meet better off than before we met.

That can be as simple as giving someone a reason to smile. The kind words and encouragement you get in return for your kindness to others will:

- Energize you throughout the day.
- Delight you and give you a sense of value and purpose.
- Create confidence in your ability to deal with anything that comes your way.
- Live a life filled with joy, peace and fulfillment.

As I was writing this bit of advice I recalled a time during my corporate career when I was feeling stressed and exhausted. Each morning during this time one of my direct reports would walk past my door and proclaim loudly "Don't talk to Dale, he's crabby." Then, while sporting a big grin, they'd poke their heads into the doorway to let me know that they were trying to cheer me up.

I couldn't help but laugh. That simple kindness restored my connection to the universe and, in doing so, set the tone for a productive, enjoyable day.

In *Influence: Science and Practice,* Robert Cialdini offers examples of how intensely beneficiaries of kindness want to reciprocate. When you make a conscious effort to leave everyone you meet better off than before you met, you create a cadre of people who'll be there for you any time you need help *as long as that isn't your motivation for doing so.*

Stop struggling

When problems surface, which they inevitably do, don't struggle. If a solution doesn't come readily to mind, ask your subconscious mind to find a solution for you. Then shift your focus to a task you can complete successfully. The next time your mind is free, the answer will surface.

That's it! That's the sum total of what you need to do at the start of your day. It takes less than five minutes to accomplish.

Throughout the day

Recognize that negative emotions are messages from the universe indicating that you're losing your connection. When these emotions surface simply ask the universe "How can I accomplish [goal] without anxiety, fear and frustration?"

The universe will respond with simple, straightforward, easily-implemented solutions—often more quickly than you imagined possible.

As I mentioned at the outset, you can enjoy a life of joy, peace and fulfillment, with only minor changes in your daily routine. The daily routine I've outlined will assure that you are more consistently and enjoyably connected to the universe. Enjoy your connection!

— *Dale Furtwengler*

About the author

Dale Furtwengler helps his clients enjoy greater personal, professional, and business success.

His internationally-acclaimed books include:

Lead a Life of Confidence
Stand Out From The Crowd
One with the Universe

Pricing for Profit
Become a Maverick
The 10-Minute Guide to Performance Appraisals
The Uniqueness Myth
Making the Exceptional Normal

Each of Dale's books provide insights into behaviors that drive, or deprive, people of the success they desire. Dale has identified these behaviors by observing incongruities between what people say and what they do. It's in these incongruities that the secrets to leading a life virtually free of fear, anxiety and frustration lie.

His books are recommended by the University of Glasgow, the University of New South Wales, the Australians Institute of Management and *Harvard Management Communication Letter*.

You can find Dale's blogs and information on how you can enjoy greater personal, professional and business success at:

PricingForProfitBook.com
TheLifeOthersDesire.com

Lead a Life of CONFIDENCE

Free yourself of fear, anxiety and frustration

EXCERPT

I want your life!

Never, in my wildest dreams, did I expect to hear these words directed to me. Yet, in the past three years, more than a half-dozen people have told me that they want my life.

When I challenge their declaration, they say:

- I want to do what I want, when I want, like you do.
- I want to avail myself of opportunities without worrying about the consequences the way you do.
- I want to take time off to travel like you do.

What they're really saying is that they want to be free of fear, anxiety and frustration, something I hadn't realized I had achieved. This realization begged the question "What is it that enables me to lead a virtually worry-free existence?"

The short answer is confidence. But that raised another question "How had I gained that confidence?" It didn't exist early in my life. In fact, despite growing up in one of the most encouraging, nurturing environments anyone could hope to have, I was a shy, insecure child. I feared meeting people because I didn't know what to say to them.

Stand Out From The Crowd

without having people point & laugh

EXCERPT

Competing desires

We human beings are a strange lot. We crave recognition, yet fear the possibility that we won't "fit in." We want to be better than others in some regard, yet recall the painful teasing we endured as children for being so.

This dichotomy of desires is evidenced in all aspects of our lives. When I work with business owners to differentiate their offerings, their primary concern is "people won't know what we do." These owners understand that they must communicate the superiority of their offerings to avoid having them viewed as commodities, but they fear that being *too* different will cost them sales.

Career-minded professionals desire recognition for their superior intellect and ability to produce results. At the same time they fear being "too far out there" or being "pigeon-holed" because either perception would limit their potential.

On a personal level we prize our individuality—the essence that makes us who we are. Yet we understand that if we don't get along with others, if we're too different, odds are we'll lead a lonely existence.

Good news

These fears are ill-founded! You can be different and still be attractive. The key is to develop insights that others value.

www.ingramcontent.com/pod-product-compliance
Lightning Source LLC
Chambersburg PA
CBHW071013040426
42443CB00007B/760